For Mary, in me ... of a lovely
day on Tristan
1994, with lo

DELIVER ME

FROM

SAFETY

by

John Woolley

Je me'expose pour me
delivrer de la securité.
Sans risque, il n'y a pas de
caractère: c'est lui,
ma protection.
Herve Bazin: *Les Bienheureux de la Désolation.*

First published in Great Britain in 1994

by

WILTON 65
Flat Top House, Bishop Wilton, York. YO4 1RY

ISBN 0 947828 42 7

Printed & Bound
by
Antony Rowe Ltd.. Chippenham. Wiltshire.

This book is dedicated
to the memory of
Florence Kate Woolley,
1882-1971.

The Author

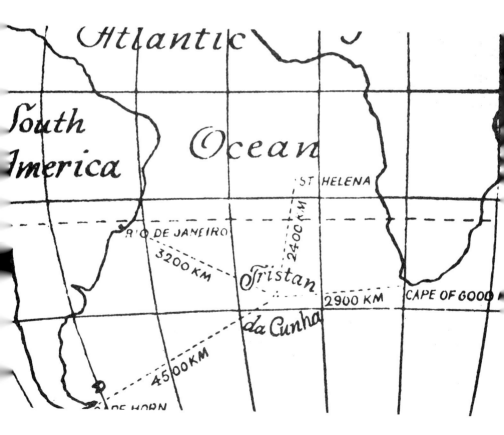

CONTENTS

Author's Note

ILLUSTRATIONS

AUTHOR's NOTE

I would like to make it clear that *Deliver me from Safety* is a personal record and does not purport to be an official history of the Denstone Expedition to Inaccessible Island.

Several acknowledgements are in the text but I would like to express my thanks for textual emendations and improvements to Paul Stephenson, John Tindale, Ian Stirling, Julian Hall and Lord and Lady Holderness.

Susie Wardell has been endlessly patient in typing and re-typing the book and the Denstone Expeditions Trust has been generous in allowing me to reproduce the photographs and maps.

My thanks are also due to the following publishers and authors:

The quotation from *The Little Black Bird Book* is reproduced by permission of Bill Oddie and Methuen, London.

The quotations from *The Penguin Cookery Book* and *The Paupers Cookbook* are reproduced by permission of Bee Nilson, Jocasta Innes and Penguin Books.

The quotations from *Les Bienheureux de La Désolation* are reproduced by permission of Hervé Bazin and Editions du Seuil.

The quotation from Ezra Pound's *Canto LXXVI* is reproduced by permission of Faber and Faber.

CHAPTER 1
Wednesday 15 September 1982

Just when we're safest, there's a sunset touch
A fancy from a flower-bell, someone's death,
A chorus ending from Euripides, -
And that's enough for fifty hopes and fears
As old and new at once as nature's self,
To rap and knock and enter in our soul,
Take hands and dance there, a fantastic ring,
Round the ancient idol, on his base again, -
The grand Perhaps ....
Browning: *Bishop Bloughram's Apology*

I woke to the sound of four little boys talking quietly in the next room. I looked at my watch. Ten to eight. Worth making a fuss? Not yet, they've only been boarding for five days and the bell is going to ring in ten minutes. I got up, washed, dressed and stuck my head round their door as the bell sounded.

"Morning boys."

"Good morning" from three voices.

"Good morning, Grandad" from the fourth, Raymond. Have to watch that one. Never mind, they look happy and are obviously settling down well.

My own youngest emerged sleepily from his room further up the corridor and he and I went through for breakfast as the four boarders started looking for their socks and ties.

I poured myself a cup of coffee and glanced at *The Times*.

"They couldn't do your Scripture prep." remarked the eleven year old.

"Could you do it?" I enquired, cautiously.

"Sort of."

I returned to *The Times*. Sylvie, my wife, poured me another cup of coffee and the post arrived. Three book catalogues, one begging letter from a well-known charity, a form for examination entries from the G.C.E. Board, one request for a reference from a former pupil and one enquiry about travel arrangements from a new parent. I took my coffee through into the study and started drafting answers for Dorothy to type later. Then I went and took Assembly - we sang a hymn and I made routine announcements.

Assembly over, I repaired to my classroom to meet 4b, who were all agog to hear about Lars Porsena of Clusium, as at least two of them were under the impression that he was a pop group. Having disillusioned them, I continued with the exploits of brave Horatius until he observed that

In yon strait path a thousand
May well be stopped by three

and brave teacher had the temerity to enquire the meaning of the word 'strait.' The answer was so obvious to half the class that they rolled their eyeballs to the heavens and sat waiting for something more interesting to turn up while the eager beavers struggled with synonyms, 'in one direction,' 'in a line,' 'not bending' ...

The tension rose as the story unfolded and I read the last stanzas without stopping and without letting my voice break.

A hand went up.

"Yes, Michael?"

"I thought you said 'arness meant armour."

"That's right."

"If he dived in the river wearing armour, 'e must 'ave soonk."

An unanswerable criticism.

Matthew came for his tutorial after break. We talked about the technique of writing A-level essays, particularly when the subject was a writer one didn't like. ('With whom one didn't empathise?') Matthew, highly intelligent but buttoned up, gave very little apart from approving nods when the value of the spoon feeding was apparent to him.

"What comes over clearly is that though you have gone through the motions quite efficiently, you find Wordsworth a bit of a dull dog."

Nod.

"I think when you are in that situation you have to look at a specific poem and ask yourself "Why did Wordsworth write on that subject and why did he treat it in that way?" Now look at what you say about 'Resolution and Independence' - "even the weather he describes is given no decoration and is not in any way unusual, and you quote

There was a roaring in the wind all night
The rain came heavily and fell in floods

then a bit later you say: 'the poem hinges on the poet's repeated and over-awed question

How is it that you live and what is it that you do?

and at the end of the next paragraph you say: 'The apparent awkwardness of the last line of the final stanza does not in any way detract from the rest of the poem: indeed the extra syllable somehow reinforces the realism

'God,' said I, 'be my help and stay secure;
I'll think of the Leech gatherer on the lonely moor!'

"Now all these are good points but I don't feel that they are connected together to give an overall impression of why Wordsworth had to write the poem in the way he did at that time in his life, particularly if you are trying to convince someone that 'Wordsworth's poetry can still have value for a largely urban community' ..."

An hour later when I had run out of justifications for my own liking for Wordsworth but had at least elicited half a dozen sentences from Matthew, there was a knock at the door. Dorothy came in, "Could you come to the telephone please. It's the headmaster of a School in Germany about an external examination candidate." I gave Matthew an essay title and followed Dorothy to the office, where I heard the bell for lunch as I finished talking to Germany.

The midday meal is always a bit of a moveable feast in the staffroom, with teachers coming in to eat where there is space available and when they can, though there seems always to be a preponderance of hungry young masters in the first twenty minutes. Sharing Eeyore's feelings about Confused Noises, I walked back to my house and chatted to my wife about the events, microcosmic and macrocosmic, of the morning.

"How are you getting on with 3a?" I enquired.

"They're still a bit lively but they're a good group as you said. There's nobody really outstanding like Christine or Anne Marie."

"What about Maria?"

My wife looked at me darkly.

"Maria is a spoilt brat."

"Have you told her?"

"No, but I have told her mother."

Relentless Gallic logic.

I went back to School for lunch.

There was one spare place at the dining table and it looked as if at least two people were finishing their dessert, so I nipped into the kitchen smartly to see if there was a queue. Miraculously, the way was clear and I helped myself to a plateful of potatoes, tinned beans (Question: 'Why isn't the chef using fresh ones at this time of year?') and a stew whose Homeric proportions seemed indicated by the size of the ladle. On re-entering the staff-room the junior member of staff at the head of the table generously moved his chair six inches so that I could squeeze behind him to occupy the vacant seat.

Conversation was raging around the sempiternal topic of how to make children who didn't want to eat attend meals. The Latin lady was explaining how she had forced John Thomas to imbibe three spoonfuls of the Homeric stew by a method more redolent of Sunday afternoon wrestling than any classical heroics. The senior games mistress suggested further physical inducements which would in her view have persuaded John Thomas to eat a whole plateful like a man - as either the inducements or the consequences of John's succumbing to them seemed equally distressing insofar as the cleanliness of the dining room was concerned, I felt it was time to intervene.

"Is there anything he likes eating?" I enquired, incautiously.

The "nothings" of half those present were balanced by the "sweeties" of the other half who took turns in administering the School Tuck Shop.

"Modern children don't like proper food."

"What is proper food?"

"If I cook a proper roast for Sunday lunch," (senior games mistress speaking) "you can bet that one third of the meat will come back in scraps. If I give them 'beefburgers' there will be hardly any waste."

I knew she was right.

"In any case" (another voice) "they prefer puddings to the main course. They'll eat anything with sugar in it."

I protested. "Hang on. Alison's main complaint about the food at Denstone is that it's 'chips with everything' and they have a choice of three different main courses there."

Senior games mistress eyed me forbiddingly; "I don't know why my goddaughter has cause for complaint in view of the fact that she made her own choice of School and anyway" (at least according me some responsibility) "none of your children have ever fussed about their food."

High praise. Flattered, I sat back and was immediately floored by an enquiry from the art master.

"How are we supposed to eat in the new dining-room?"

Feebly: "Well, with knife, fork and spoon, I would hope?"

Art master, aggro creeping in and beard jutting forth:

"That's not what I mean. Are we going to eat with the children every day at a certain place at a certain time?"

"Of course not. I would hope that the whole atmosphere of school lunches will change with the presence of the staff at their own dining table and certain members on a rota scattered about among the children's tables ..." I continued to explain and the conversation and comments continued to flow.

At about ten past two the biology master bustled in and asked me for the key to the Land Rover because he was going sailing with some 5th form boys.

Accorded.

That meant that I had to walk down to the games field through the mud of two fields, knowing that I would have to come back again in time to clean up and teach last lesson at twenty to four. On the field there were vague signs of activity which increased frenetically as my approach was perceived and as I became progressively more adjacent. I was accosted by one of the junior games masters.

"I can't mark the field because there's no water in the trough."

"Have you tried the trough on the far side?"

"It's been empty since August."

"Have you asked George why the water isn't on?"

"No, because it was on last week."

"Right, I'll walk over and ask him. Almost certainly it's because his sheep are out and he thinks we don't need water, though God knows. I've told him often enough."

I made my way through shoals of perspiring bodies and tried to reason with the logic of the North Yorkshire farmer, still giving nowt for nowt, despite the fat years of Common Market pampering.

Then back up the hill, puffing disgracefully as I reached my front gate.

A few minutes later I faced 3a who clearly felt that last period on a Wednesday afternoon was a bit much and that it was up to me to provide some kind of entertainment which would at least pass the time as pleasantly as possible in view of the unfortunate circumstances. We had reached Chaucer and I copied three stanzas of *Troilus and Criseyde* on to the blackboard.

A hand went up.

"What does 'swich' mean?"

"Such."

"Why is it spelt with a 'y' instead of an 'i' in line five?" (Maria)

"Because the language was still evolving and spelling was different in different parts of the country so nobody was very worried about it."

A gleam came into Graham's eye.

"You mean spelling didn't matter?"

"Didn't, Graham, not doesn't. But spelling was still quite an individual matter even in Shakespeare's day, as was pronunciation. Now, can we have a translation of the first stanza -

And down from thennes faste he gan avyse

This litel spot of erthe, that with the se
Embraced is ... "

Gradually a little animation began to creep into the sodden masses of protoplasm before me until the arrival of the 'bus, as usual five minutes early, drove all thoughts of further study from their minds. I dismissed them and plodded wearily homewards.

The young men were already clustering around my wife in the kitchen, anxious for tuck. I watched as she carefully divided Mark's cake and couldn't resist offering the suggestion that if she let one of them cut it with the proviso that the others chose first, she would get four exactly equal segments.

She rewarded me with one of her looks and I retreated to my study where, fortified with a can of beer, I marked books until about twenty-five to six when the youngest opened the door and hissed "Come on, Dad - it's 'Will o the Wisp.' " I went.

Then I watched the news. Then the telephone rang. (I don't know why I have such a passion for watching/ listening to the six o'clock news and my children certainly can't understand it, but they weren't brought up during the early forties - it still irritates me, however, when people telephone while they ought to be watching The News - I can't help feeling that they must have got their priorities somewhat misdirected.)

By the time I had finished dealing with the enquiries about travel arrangements for the Christmas holidays, examination choices for the summer examinations and had agreed to extra visits for Sonia and Elsbeth because the parents were splitting up, the electric bell was sounding for prep. I went and supervised.

At eight o'clock I walked home in the darkness to find the small boys, pink, clean and cat-licked in their dressing gowns sitting watching something relatively anodyne on the television. I cast a hopeful glance at the *Radio Times* but it looked like another non-viewing night. It was Hachis Parmentier for dinner and conversation at the table revolved around the eleven year old's impressions of his first week up in the senior school. He seemed to be surviving the changeover from one single teacher to ten different ones without too much difficulty and the fact that he was also talking to his headmaster did not seem too inhibiting. Only two comments led to sudden parental exchanges in French but there was a knowledgeable glint in the youngest's eye which suggested that 'pas devant' was not going to be a viable proposition for much longer. After the second of these exchanges he decided to change the subject.

"What time are we leaving on Saturday?" he asked.

"We have to be at the Range gate at nine. Can we have a picnic please?" I asked my wife.

"Have you got a gun?"

"Not this time. I'll be driving beaters about and flanking. It's Tom's home moor so there should be plenty of birds about."

"C'est Tom le garde-chasse?"

"Oui."

"N'oublie pas de lui rappeler qu'on a mangé le dernier lièvre."

"I think they all know that you prefer hare to grouse, my love."

The telephone rang. For once I had finished my plate. The local rugby club, wanting players on Saturday. I agreed, with reservations.

Putting the receiver down, I decided that I had done enough marking for one day and cast an eye over my library to find something I wanted to read or re-read. Ten minutes later I had finally picked out one of my oldest favourites *Le Hussard sur le Toit*. It was lamentable that I had taken so long to decide and also, I thought, somewhat distressing that with about five thousand books to choose from, my choice nowadays inevitably settled on one from about twenty-five, ignoring all the others.

I mentioned the fact to my wife who gave me a praying mantis-like look before observing sweetly

"Il ne meurt jamais que les plus malades."

I poured myself a whisky and buried myself in Giono until bedtime.

That was it. So ended Wednesday, 15 September, another fairly normal day in a place where I had lived for nineteen years. I was in my mid-forties, had been headmaster for ten, and I slept soundly.

On Thursday, 16 September at 0750 hours, the telephone rang and when I picked it up, a voice said

"John? Can you take three months off and go to the South Atlantic with the Denstone Expedition to Inaccessible Island, starting on 1 October?"

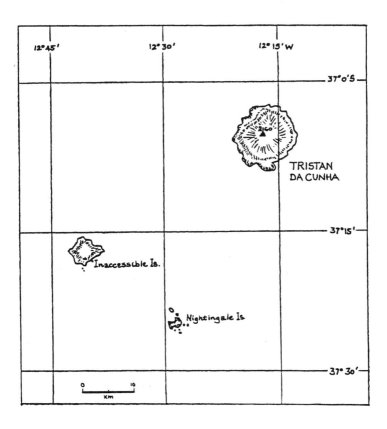

The three islands of Tristan

CHAPTER 2

GOING

Better is the end of a thing than the beginning thereof.
Book of Proverbs

There were, of course, certain people to be asked and Mike was kind enough to give me twenty-four hours to decide. But perhaps I should explain at this point that I did know what he was talking about because I had been hearing about the Denstone Expedition to Inaccessible Island for the previous four-and-a-half years without ever having been privileged to receive such an invitation.

Mike Swales is a very old friend. Some years older than myself, our lives have followed somewhat similar patterns in that we both went to the same prep. school, the same public school, did our National Service in different branches of the Armed Services, both went to Cambridge reading different subjects in different Colleges and both - after various periods abroad - returned to one of our Alma Maters to teach. We then remained there for very lengthy periods. Friends though we are, we have not overlapped, which probably explains why our friendship has continued to flourish, a friendship strengthened when our wives struck up an immediate rapport.

The most significant of Mike's adventures abroad occurred when he went with the Expedition to Gough Island, 200 miles to the south of Tristan, as ornithologist in 1955/56: in a consequential visit to Tristan da Cunha, he was deeply affected by the character of that lonely community, certainly the loneliest community on earth, and it may even have been at that time that he conceived the idea of exploring Inaccessible, one of the two uninhabited islands lying within twenty miles of Tristan: [*see Map 1a*] the other, Nightingale, is, or was, visited about twice a year by the Tristan islanders, whereas visits to Inaccessible were very rare and always of a very short duration.

If one looks at a map of the South Atlantic and draws a line from Cape Town to Buenos Aires one meets the three islands about half-way across, eighteen hundred miles from Cape Town and thirteen hundred from St Helena to the north.[*See map 1b*] Tristan itself was discovered in 1506 by the Portuguese navigator Tristao da Cunha. In 1816 it was formally annexed by the British who feared that the French might occupy it in an attempt to organise the escape of Napoleon, imprisoned on St Helena. One of the garrison, Corporal William Glass, a Scot, decided he would like to remain when the garrison was withdrawn in 1821 and he was joined by a few kindred spirits. The present population of some three hundred descends from them and from men who have been shipwrecked or who have chosen to settle there during the nineteenth century.

When Denstone was approaching its centenary year Mike had suggested an Expedition to do a scientific, ecological and cartographic survey of Inaccessible Island which would be carried out entirely by teachers and former and present pupils of the College, to celebrate that event. He had received the enthusiastic support of the new headmaster, Tim Beynon, who had been given permission to join the Expedition under Mike's leadership by the Governors, but Tim had now been obliged to withdraw in totally unforeseeable circumstances. On various occasions during the previous four years when I had volunteered my services as non-scientific cook, I had been rejected fairly contemptuously because of the 'non-scientific' label: I hope it was only human to feel some residual self-satisfaction that they were now calling on me, totally ignorant as I was of all the detail, when there remained less than two weeks before departure. However, there were certain little domestic difficulties to sort out and to these I now turned my mind.

I met the first as Sylvie advanced majestically into the kitchen about to prepare my breakfast coffee. Whether it was the frontage afforded by her nightgown or some instinct which warned me to be blunt, I don't know, but I decided on the direct assault.

"That was Mike and he wants me to go to Inaccessible on the

first of October. I would be away for three months." It may be only my faulty memory because things began to move so fast from then onwards, but my recollection is that she replied almost unhesitatingly, "You must go."

My own reaction was to start raising all the difficulties which she, the School and my own classes might then encounter. Majestically she brushed them all away. Some of their brush-offs were so libellous as to be unrepeatable, but even she admitted that I could not depart without the agreement of four other people, the first being my co-Principal, Clare White. This is not a book about my School, nor about Clare White, though I have every intention of writing such a book someday: suffice it to say that her immediate reaction when I broke the news - with some trepidation - was the same as my wife's (anybody would have thought that they were all anxious to get rid of me!) It was a generous and gallant agreement because she was not fully fit and had to put off a serious operation pending my return which put her out of action for the whole of the spring term.

My deputy-head, Alex Gregg, listened carefully to my somewhat simplistic account of the problems involved, and accepted the challenge almost without demur, and similarly my eldest son, Simon, agreed to return immediately from his beloved Midi after about one minute's explanation on the telephone.

By this time it was about midday and that left one major problem: my senior English mistress, who had taught me at the age of thirteen and had retired secretly at the end of the previous summer term when I had taken over most of her classes. Now I went to see her, trepidating excessively, to see if, after ten days retirement she would re-emerge until Christmas, because there was nobody in the world to whom I would have entrusted those classes except Daisy Hardy. It is a tribute to her character that having listened to my case in somewhat awful silence, her first reaction was to comment on how she would be laughed at in the village, and her second to request that could she please teach in her own (former) classroom and not mine. We drank glasses of sherry and I was enjoined to keep a diary during my absence. I agreed.

My teaching that afternoon remains vague in my memory: 4b were still shell-shocked from the previous day's blow by blow *Horatius* and I think we managed to pass the time with verbs and nouns, a part of the syllabus which we teachers are no longer allowed to call 'grammar' but can excuse under the label 'syntax.' I imagined how various MPs and members of HMG might get caught under the new alternative heading and repressed my baser instincts.

There was also the new 1a, including my own youngest, handing in their Scripture prep and listening to a discourse on tribal development in ancient Palestine. Maybe they knew something was up because my youngest had picked up a hint at breakfast or during the course of the day. Certainly they were well-behaved, as were our little boarders after half-past four, and the vital discussion took place at about 7.15 pm when I rang Tim Beynon, whose place I would be taking, and who was very encouraging and enthusiastic. At about 9 pm I rang Mike and said "Yes." Then I stayed awake most of the night.

For the next few days things moved sometimes very quickly, sometimes apparently slowly. I knew that Mike's wife, Elizabeth, was not at all well, so I hesitated to telephone too often with what might seem irrelevant and unnecessary queries, though a large number began to accumulate. I had received very quickly a large sheaf of instructions and papers and these filled a great deal of my 'spare' time. I had filled in a medical questionnaire from Dr. Nick Hall, the deputy leader, and went off for a medical with my own GP, who was not only a friend but one whose children I had taught. Apart from suppressing the odd detail about my back, which has given me trouble on and off (but mostly off) since I fractured a vertebra playing rugby in the Army when I was nineteen, I was completely honest, though I certainly made Bob Paul aware of the necessity of passing me fit and giving me the required inoculation jabs. He complied in good-humoured fashion with a warning about incipient hernia, an optimistic forecast about the eventual benefit to my pot-belly and an irreverent speculation as to how long the 'drying-off' period would take!

Thus heartened I had a call from Mike on 21 September to say that the Expedition would have no air mattresses and no kit-bags and would I please do something about it through my important contacts on the Whitby Fish Quay. (I have a regular 'exchange and mart' system which produces a lot of fresh fish and shellfish against rabbits from my twelve-bore.) The latter failed to produce much, but a friendly parent who runs a Sports Shop in Whitby did the impossible and had all the material delivered to Derby Station by the appointed time.

By the 24 September I was writing in my diary: 'trying to do five jobs at the same time is slightly more restful than trying to do three - you wait for the problems to crop up in each job more patiently and if you know the first three jobs anyway, you can prepare for those problems more in advance. The trouble is I know so little knowledge about the problems on Inaccessible and I keep having to ring Mike about fiddling details. The other problem is passing on the essential information to the people who will be doing my job here - I am sure they will do a good job but they are inclined to waste time on minutiae without realising the enormous goodwill that exists among the children - I hope it exists among the members of the Expedition!'

The following day was my forty-sixth birthday and my important contacts on the Whitby Fish Quay, having adjourned to Jim Mortlock's *Fisherman's Tavern* for pre-prandial beer, were pleased to serenade me with a "Happy Birthday" chorus which caused the odd raised eyebrow from the end-of-season middle-aged(!) visitors walking along the pier. At a family dinner party that evening my brother, who was home on leave from Bahrain, did a sterling job in convincing my mother that what I was doing was reasonable, though there was a pregnant silence at one moment when she remarked "Of course you won't be doing anything silly like mountaineering, will you dear? ... After all you don't know anything about it."

On the 27th Simon got stuck in Calais on his way home because bad weather had grounded the hovercraft, and my brother and I eventually set off to pick him up from York where he arrived at midnight. He talked all the way home and once there we sat up for hours listening to him and asking questions.

For the next day my diary reads: 'At about 7 pm, Mike rang to say that Elizabeth's condition was so serious that the doctors had advised him that he ought not to consider leading the Expedition.

Would I still go?

I asked for time to think, which he immediately granted.

Family said "Go." Tim Beynon said "Go."

I couldn't contact the new leader, Nick Hall, but eventually rang Mike to say "Yes," providing Nick and the other scientific leaders agreed. Hope to God I will not be utterly useless - they seem to think I have some kind of organisational capacity because I have been a headmaster for ten years. If only they knew! Must go on writing UCCA reports.'

On Wednesday 29 September I stopped teaching at lunchtime and watched rugby and hockey matches against visiting Schools on our games field: I must have been preoccupied because I can't remember whether we won or lost. Daisy Hardy arrived the following morning to take over my classes and as I had said goodbye to the School in Assembly on the Wednesday, I was free to make last minute purchases, to nag my wife about sewing name tags into garments and to pack.

We had been given a personal allowance of some ten books apart from bird books, cookery books, botanical guides and diaries. Somewhat selfishly, because they were useless to the rest of the Expedition, I could not resist *Le Rouge et le Noir* and *La Chartreuse de Parme*. In the end I regretted the latter because of the forgotten 'longeurs' about two-thirds of the way through, though the former undoubtedly steeled my resolve during the voyage from Cape Town to Tristan. I took a complete Shakespeare in very fine print which I used a little, as did other, sometimes unlikely members of the Expedition, and two Dickens novels *Bleak House* and *Our Mutual Friend*, the latter largely because it was an A-level set book for the following summer. I also took Steinbeck's *Log from the Sea of Cortez*, but eventually left that at Denstone when I realised just how overweight we were all going to be.

I had chosen an old cassette recorder from the infinite number discarded by former pupils, and having equipped myself with a supply of batteries, raided Simon's supply of cassettes which, according to the labels, gave me about two dozen Bach, Beethoven and Mozart works from which to choose. What was my dismay some three weeks later when, preparing to listen to a Mozart Quartet and inserting the cassette in the recorder, I found myself listening to the miaulings of some Swedish pop group artist with a totally unpronounceable name. Luckily only about three of the chosen two dozen came into this category. Perhaps I should say "luckily for me."

On the 1 October Simon drove me to Scarborough Station to catch the early train to York from where I would proceed to Denstone. From the weight of my suitcase I concluded that not only was I grossly overweight but also grossly unfit. Mike, who met me at Uttoxeter, made light of the first problem and made arrangements to confirm the latter by having photographs taken not only of my belly, but those of the whole Expedition. I spent the day listening to a somewhat bewildering series of instructions and in marking and packing all the kit supplied for the Expedition. Luckily, my daughter Alison had been excused school for the second half of the day and she was a great help while I was getting to know the other members. Now that Mike was no longer going I could claim acquaintance only with Nick Hall (and that was on the strength of two telephone conversations) and the first thing I learnt on arrival was that I was now the deputy leader.

I met David Gilfillan, the youngest member, still in his 5th form year at Denstone, who doled out to me all the various bits of clothing and bedding, and I then went off to a local pub with Nick and Alison.

How do you sum up the character of someone with whom you are going to share the responsibility for the well-being of ten other people and direct them to carry out a difficult task (about which you know very little yourself) during a period of some three months, over a pub lunch after an hour's acquaintance? I don't think I tried very hard: I listened to Nick swapping repartee with Alison and realised that he was more than competent to cope with my daughter and that she liked him. Such a combination is so rare that my respect for him instilled itself immediately and was rarely shaken during the ensuing adventure.

Our retreat to the pub was not just an appreciation that we had got to get to know each other very quickly: it was also a retreat from the doom-laden atmosphere surrounding Mike on that day and the succeeding one, an atmosphere which I think only Nick and I were aware of, because Mike concealed it so cheerfully from all the other members. The Denstone Expedition to Inaccessible Island had filled a large part of his life for the previous four years, and to have to renounce participation with five days to go must have been a bitter frustration. He did his best to give us all the background information he could, while knowing that we would not (could not) run things altogether in the way which he had envisaged. As the departure of the Expedition had been postponed some eighteen months previously for financial reasons, there was a certain urgency pertaining to our departure on this occasion whatever the circumstances, and Nick and I came to an appreciation of the situation very quickly, even though at that stage we did not realise the full consequences of our decision.

I met Richard Preece, the Invertebrate Zoologist, in the afternoon: my recollection is of a rather large gentle gentleman with an inordinate amount of personal sleeping baggage, who demanded a special allowance on the flight to Cape Town because he was carrying more scientific equipment than anybody else. Then there was the other Richard, Dick Holt, who had just left Denstone having gained a place at St Catherine's College, Cambridge, to read Natural Sciences in 1983; quiet and reserved, it was difficult to make an instant rapport though I felt an immediate sympathy for him when I learnt his father was a schoolmaster.

The odd man out in all the turmoil was the other Mike - odd man out only in the sense that he had no connection with Denstone. Mike Fraser was a Scottish protégé of Tim Beynon who had been engaged at five days notice to take the ornithological place of Mike Swales: as both ornithologists (Tim was the other) had now dropped out, he spent a large part of the day closeted in conference with them. He had never been out of Great Britain before but very luckily was in possession of a valid passport, and I was much cheered to learn that he had spent a year reading English literature at some Scottish University where it had proved possible to change to biology when he realised where his true interests lay.

There was another David, who had just left Denstone, and to whom I had apparently been introduced on a previous parental visit Alison-wards: David Briggs was well-built, blond and good-looking, and I understood why my daughter dug me in the ribs and hissed "Surely you remember meeting David last summer?" I flannelled out of that one and met Ian Best, who had also just left the College and appeared rather vague but was, according to my limited information, an excellent practical physicist. Ian's expensive camera eventually provided the Expedition with many of its best slides and he was to spend many an hour struggling with the intricacies of the wind generator and arguing with Richard Holt about what to do next, but I had little time to appreciate his worth on that day or indeed till much later.

The two late arrivals were Clive Siddall and Joe Dakin. The former had completed two years at the University of Leeds, reading Mechanical Engineering, but had been given a year off to undertake the task of making the map of Inaccessible, which was an essential part of the Expedition's project, on which he had been originally engaged as the 'Assistant.' He had now been given the full responsibility for the map but his main preoccupation at our first meeting seemed to be about the quality and quantity of food which would be available on Inaccessible. Having had my briefing and seen the ration lists, I found little to reassure him, even if I had had the time. The same limitation applied to Joe Dakin, another young man who had just left Denstone, but who obviously had important social engagements in the College that evening! He was to prove invaluable in all the manual/ physical/ practical necessities of the Expedition and he was Clive's assistant in the completion of the map. I sometimes wonder now if their successful association was a result of their late arrival on that first day, because it was rarely possible to make contact with them individually from then on.

Nick and the two Mikes went off to an important trustees Meeting (Mike Fraser not to attend but to pick up further ornithological gen from Tim when occasion offered). The young men went off in various College directions leaving semi-organised chaos in Mike Swales' house and I went off with Nick's wife, Sarah, plus Alison, to the village pub because none of us were hungry and we couldn't face supper in Hall. The village pub was not pleasant but at least it offered a chance for Sarah to get to know the new man who would be supporting her husband in what was beginning to look like a fairly desperate venture. Intelligent, intellectually taut, a practising GP in her own right and highly competent, she and I seemed to understand each other very quickly, and Alison's presence was an enormous help, not just because she prevented the voicing of our now deeply-felt fears, but because on that evening (if not the following morning) Alison was full of confidence which neither Sarah nor I wished to shake.

Then there was the meeting of the Expedition members in Mike's house. Mike spoke well about what he could envisage in general and Nick, as far as I can remember, talked about the medical risks we were undertaking. They had warned me to expect to say a few words which I devoted to my fairly total incompetence but also, particularly, my non-scientific background. Perhaps I failed to emphasise that I had had some experience in getting on with people in various walks of life, which explains some of our minor misunderstandings during the flight to Cape Town.

It must have been a deeply distressing meeting for Mike, well though he gave encouragement to the young men whom he had chosen and who had been expecting to be led by him until five days previously. We retired eventually to the Sanatorium where the whole Expedition was expected to 'get an early night.' At least two members dribbled in at 2 am (quite quietly) but I was unable to sleep anyway, as I think was Nick.

The following morning we repaired to Hall for breakfast. I chatted to Alison in desultory fashion (she was busy doing her prefectorial duty marking off members of Woodard House 'present') and pecked at the scrambled egg which I couldn't eat. We appeared at the right time for a photo-call, but the member of staff designated to carry out the exercise failed to turn up until some forty-five minutes later, an inadvertence which did little to add to anybody's confidence in the organisation behind the Expedition, especially in view of the members' psychological state at that particular time. The whole school turned out to bid us "Bon Voyage" and I remember walking down the drive with an increasingly pale Alison beside me and a loaded minibus and lots of people in front. The only thing I remember saying was "Don't forget I'm doing this because I want to" (a maxim I have often had to repeat to myself on a grouse moor on a wet autumn day), but I don't think she was in a fit state to comprehend and she fled precipitately once we had said goodbye, to be comforted by her understanding housemistress.

The photos and farewells seemed to go on forever and then there was another (planned) stop to say real farewells two hundred yards down the College drive and out of sight of the School: a fortunate piece of planning because we had neglected to pick up our picnic lunches. The fact that they were eventually remembered was a cause of some dismay to the younger generation who had experienced College picnic lunches before. The journey to Heathrow seemed interminable and I was grateful for the challenge when Mike eventually asked me to take over and be responsible for getting the baggage through 'Check-In.' Though several of the younger members who had been flying in and out of the country for most of their lives had their own ideas, I managed to get all the baggage together and to dole out certain items as 'personal luggage.' I then fixed what I hoped was an appealing gaze on the South African Airways lovely, as ton after ton of kit-bags, coffer-bags, boxes and other impedimenta were heaped on the remorseless weighing machine and she checked over our ten tickets.

Having worked it all out she said:

"You are ninety-two kilograms overweight" ....

"I hope you realise the scientific importance of this Expedition," I replied. "It is going under the auspices of the South African Government, as well as the Royal Geographical Society, and several of our suppliers did not deliver until yesterday morning, which made it impossible to send the goods in advance by sea. By the way, how much would we have to pay for the excess?"

She smiled sweetly. "Nine hundred and twenty pounds sterling."

I blanched. She smiled again. "I think we can distribute your excess over some of the other passengers who are carrying much less. Perhaps you would like to leave it with me?" I left it and fled, dragging importunate Expedition members with me and saying goodbye to Mike and the Denstone Bursar, who had shared the driving on the way down, rather abruptly but probably fortunately, such was my haste to get through Customs before she changed her mind. Our seats in the aircraft were dotted about but I had arranged to sit with Nick so that we could exchange ideas and information during the flight. Our take-off involved a protracted ascent of the runway, ending with a lift-off which seemed to brush the perimeter fence with our wheels: a reluctant air passenger at the best of times, I was little cheered by the gasps of Nick on one side and my unknown neighbour on the other. Maybe it was our excess ninety-two kilos.

The first idea which Nick and I exchanged, an idea with which our neighbour found instant accord, was large whiskies and after that we felt better. My neighbour, who had one leg entirely encased in plaster, was a South African citizen who had been salmon-fishing in Scotland despite the broken leg. When we had explained what we and the Expedition were preparing to do, he thumped the fragile table in front of him joyfully, said that he wished he was going with us, and commanded more whisky from a passing steward in magisterial fashion.

By this time, though we had a long and useful talk, both Nick and I had had little sleep or food for the previous thirty-six hours and we both formed a high opinion of the South African cuisine and of the standard of comfort, which allowed us both to get at least four hours sleep before landing for refuelling at Abidjan at about four o'clock in the morning. I went to sleep thinking about my wife and family, particularly the former, and reciting the last stanza of Donne's great *Song* to myself and to her:

> *Let not thy divining heart*
> *Forethinke me any ill,*
> *Destiny may take thy part*
> *And may thy fears fulfill;*
> *But think that wee*
> *Are but turned aside to sleepe;*
> *They who one another keepe*
> *Alive, n'er parted be.'*

All we had said at 6 am the previous morning was something like "Merde" and possibly "Bye."

*   *   *

The plan was to fly to Johannesburg where we would be met by my friend and former pupil Philip Hayton and his wife, who would help us to transfer to the 'plane for Cape Town. At Cape Town we would spend three days picking up more essential equipment before embarking on the South African government's Antarctic survey ship *Agulhas* for a voyage to Tristan which could last anything between a week and a fortnight, depending on weather conditions. We didn't know exactly when the Royal Navy were going to pick us up but just prior to Christmas seemed fairly logical if we were to be home for the second of January ...

If I had been doing my job, I ought to have circulated a bit more in the hour or two prior to our landing in Johannesburg but this was difficult because of all the other passengers in the way. Like Nick, I had also become aware that we had to do the same trick with our overweight baggage in Johannesburg that we had performed at Heathrow, and that on this occasion the Bursar was not in the wings with a cheque book. We actually planned transferring all the impedimenta to a hired van if the Airport authorities proved obdurate and using our BarclayCards to drive from Johannesburg to Cape Town, while the rest of the Expedition continued by air. When we landed at Jan Smuts Airport, the first problem was again to assemble everybody so that we looked like an Expedition, but once we had accomplished this (considerable) feat and were duly standing in a very long slow-moving queue, the Invertebrate Zoologist found an overpowering desire to pee which he accomplished while I was explaining to a Customs official about our photographic/ scientific/ surveying equipment. The official waved us through in lordly fashion but something had been left behind, not the Invertebrate Zoologist, but the geological hammers, which had been considered lethal weapons at Heathrow and could only therefore be transported in the pilot's cabin - so I had to make my way back through all the rigmarole to reclaim them! When I emerged triumphant finally, I was greeted by a smiling Philip Hayton, together with his wife, Thelma, and their two-year-old son, James. They, together with an old Denstonian, helped us to wheel our mountains of luggage to the other end of the Airport in the increasing heat of the near midday sun, and I watched as another attractive young lady with the Airport label on a plastic sticker at her lapel did her sums, listened to my spiel, smiled semi-seductively and passed us through. One of the young men enquired as to why I was sweating so profusely, particularly as Jan Smuts was such a pretty girl ...

Philip and Thelma swept us off to a hotel for refreshments, an enterprise which was a pleasant relief from the rigours of air confinement, though we managed to mislay three members in the process. Despite my anxieties about their welfare, we managed to relax for an hour and I exchanged news with our hosts about events during the years intervening since I had last seen them. Then back to Jan Smuts where our missing three had already proceeded through the embarkation zone in the ever-increasing heat. No seats were allotted for the flight from Jo'burg to Cape Town and I found myself between a well-developed but unknown young lady who had the window seat and Richard Preece who was next to the gangway.

During take-off the young lady instructed us as to the disposal of our hand-baggage, being particularly concerned with Richard's peat-corer, leaning forward to emphasise her point in a way which made her decollétage most striking. It was possibly this sideshow which caused another young member to approach down the gangway during the flight and ask where he had seen Philip Hayton on the telly?

"He's the BBC's permanent reporter in South Africa," I told him.

"Why did *he* come to meet us?" was the next query.

"Because I used to teach him History" I replied.

"Yes, but why did he bring his wife?"

"I suppose because I used to teach her French." He blasphemed and departed reluctantly, I sat back and wondered whether Philip and Thelma were enhancing my status more than the vision to my right.

The vision proved most informative about herself and the view from the aircraft: the moment which remains particularly in my memory is when she called our attention to the Drakensberg mountains below, and Richard Preece leaning across me and peering downwards observed that they were 'interesting structures:' as I was sipping a glass of beer at that moment the consequences for the passengers immediately in front of me might have been unfortunate without the height of the intervening seat but as it was, there was only a temporary moment of confusion and our self-possessed vision seemed unaware of its cause, possibly because it later emerged that she was not quite seventeen and on her way back to school!

At Cape Town Airport we were met by the Expedition's honorary liaison officer, Bernard Hill of Safmarine and his wife Brenda, backed up by Don McClachlan representing Tristan Investments Ltd. During the next three days Bernard and Don were to prove endlessly patient, helpful and hospitable, apart from giving Nick and me quiet comfort in the shocks which were awaiting us. Two 'Combis' (half passenger, half luggage vans) had been hired by Bernard to take us and our baggage to the Helmsley Hotel, a comfortable rambling establishment where memories of the Union Castle Line abounded and where the length of the dinner menu immediately made a great impression on our members.

After dinner, we had a meeting in one of the Hotel's lounges in which a general discussion revealed some discontent with the inadequacies of the supplies, particularly on the material side. I drew up a list of requirements for Bernard Hill and Safmarine, and perhaps missed out on the chance to remedy some of the deficiencies on the catering list, being still blissfully ignorant of the nature of life on Tristan. Other sources of dissension became evident, the main one being mistrust of Nick's and particularly my own capacity to lead the Expedition in the way in which the younger members had expected it would be led.

Knowing very well the innate conservatism of the young, I could only sympathise, though it was more difficult to combat the resentment of one or two 'old' hands at the arrival of a newcomer who had not gone through two or three years of preparation. Ten years of being a headmaster undoubtedly helped me in dealing with the authorities during the next fortnight, but were of little use in impressing half a dozen unknown young men already suffering from the normal recalcitrance of those who had just left school. I felt even more aware of my inadequacies as I went to bed that night but exhaustion and the luxury of a single room combined to give me a good night's rest.

If we thought we had problems in getting to Cape Town, Nick and I were made brutally aware of our real ones during 4 October and in the succeeding two days. Our first visit on the 4th, under the faithful guidance of Don McClachlan, was to the South African Government Antarctic Survey Ice-breaker *Agulhas*, which hopefully was to convey us to Inaccessible, and her formidable Captain Leith. Nick and I had chosen David Briggs and Joe Dakin to accompany us, as being the two who knew most about the eight tons of supplies which had preceded us to Cape Town, and which now reposed on the back of a lorry on the quayside. We had been assured that there was a continuous night-watch, but we both had pangs of horror as we comprehended the full enormity of the ease with which our supplies were available to petty theft. We made our way high into the towering superstructure of the *Agulhas* and into the cabin of Captain Leith where, after one dismissive glance at our young men lounging in his armchairs, he made his position clear.

"My Government has told me that you do NOT have scientific status because there are not enough qualified scientists among your members. I will do everything I can to help you but if one word of my assistance leaks out, I will be inundated by requests for help of a similar nature from every school in South Africa, none of which has yet had the imagination to project such an Expedition as yours - thank God!"

He then told us about the rules and regulations of behaviour in *Agulhas*, all of which seemed to me utterly reasonable in view of the incredible risks which he was incurring every time he took his ship to sea.

"My job," he then added, "is to convey you to Tristan da Cunha, not to Inaccessible Island. If weather conditions dictate an early landing on Inaccessible, in order to allow me to continue with my scientific programme, I will of course assist you to the best of my ability." Was there a suspicion of a wink in my direction as he uttered this last sentence? I prayed that there was.

I continued to pray following our next meeting, which was with Peter Day, an ex-Administrator of Tristan and now Managing Director of Tristan Investments, the company which owned the two fishing boats and the crayfish freezer factory on Tristan.

The two facts which Peter Day impressed on us were that we would be crazy to land on Inaccessible without knowing how we were to be taken off (we didn't), and that if we had a crisis which we had caused by our own negligence while on Inaccessible, the cost to his company for every day that one of his fishing boats was not fishing, was two-and-a-half thousand pounds. (Nick and I fingered our Barclaycards doubtfully.)

We had been told that the Royal Navy had given a verbal assurance that we would be picked up by one of their vessels and the tragic Falklands conflict had at least had one beneficiary in that the Expedition could count on greatly increased Royal Navy traffic in the South Atlantic. We had also been told that if the Royal Navy did not fulfil expectations there was no problem because we could charter the *Aragonite*, a small vessel based on St Helena. Whatever happened, we had been assured that we would be home for the 2nd of January, and this was particularly important for Nick who was to take up a hospital post later in that month, for Richard Preece who had a series of lectures to deliver at Cambridge in the Lent Term, and for myself who had been generously granted a three month (but no more) sabbatical by my long-suffering Trustees.

It emerged from our conversation with Peter Day that the *Aragonite* was at present in Cape Town and thither the indefatigable Don McClachlan conducted us, so that we could at least make sure of our 'fail-safe' procedure. Our conversation with the junior officers on the poop deck made it clear that they had no knowledge of a possible charter prior to Christmas, and it was a subdued party who returned to the Helmsley Hotel for a very late lunch. Bernard Hill offered four of us hospitality at his house prior to dinner that evening and we passed some time pleasantly stalking chameleons in his garden. On our return to the Helmsley we were met by Eddie Viljoen, to whom we were going to supply a certain number of stamp covers with our own unique GPO cachet and, as this transaction was to pay for the Expedition's stay at the Helmsley Hotel, our discussion was protracted over some three and a half hours.

Eddie had been to both Gough Island and Tristan and had considerable experience of the philatelic trade. Stamps are a most important part of the Tristan economy and the news that Inaccessible Island was to have its own official Post Office for the duration of our stay made Eddie's business nose twitch so violently that he was prepared to advance us enough money to pay the hotel bill, even though he was more aware than we were that our chances of getting on and off Inaccessible successfully were no more than 50/50 at that stage. We drank a lot of beer and missed dinner. Nick phoned Mike Swales at Denstone to voice our anxieties and later was kind enough to open one of his duty-free bottles of whisky, so again I slept soundly, both in his room and my own.

The following day was 'planned,' in that the three senior experts were off to the University of Cape Town to talk about surveying equipment and ornithological things, whilst the rest went on a mini-bus tour of the Cape. I held the fort at the Helmsley, which was probably a good thing because Don turned up with a telex from the company controlling *Aragonite*: its import was that the *Aragonite* was not available for charter before February and that we would be well advised to take supplies to last until then. When Nick returned from the tour of the Cape, we looked at each other and agreed that our Barclaycards would not extend to this kind of extra expenditure, and that evening, so convinced I was that I would never see her again, I wrote a letter to my wife which has since mysteriously disappeared. We also agreed to phone Mike again that evening, this time with me on the end, the object being to make it clear that if we could not get some definite promise from the Royal Navy, we would be obliged to take advantage of the two known sailing dates from Tristan prior to Christmas - i.e.. the *Agulhas* round the 3 November (which could take any number) and the *Tristania II* round about the 16 December, with room for about five or six. Anybody leaving on *Agulhas* would have only about three weeks on Inaccessible, those leaving on *Tristania II* (one of Peter Day's fishing boats) would have about seven weeks.

That evening we entertained Mr. and Mrs. Day and Mr. and Mrs. Viljoen and, as a result of Peter Day's representations, my call to Mike was slightly acrimonious and excessively prolonged: I still cringe at the memory of what I said to one of my oldest and closest friends but I still think I was right to express what I felt about the welfare of the Expedition members and my own. If only the Royal Navy could have been more explicit!

CHAPTER 3

'... GOING ...'

It is a strange thing that in sea-voyages, where there is nothing to be seen but sky and sea, men should make diaries, but in land-travel, wherein so much is to be observed, for the most part they omit it; as if chance were fitter to be registered than observation.

Francis Bacon: Of Travel

During the morning of the 6 October we made final packing arrangements and chatted to Dr. Brendan Halpin who was coming to Tristan on the *Agulhas* for a three week veterinary check up of the domestic animals on behalf of HM Government. His knowledge of the world, his sense of humour and his acquaintance with many varied countries were a source of entertainment for much of the voyage, and Nick and I appreciated his wise counsel once he realised the full implications of our undertaking. All our new friends turned up at the dock to see us off, and even if they were not our nearest and dearest, their presence added an extra touch of feeling to what is anyway an emotional occasion, the departure of a ship for a prolonged voyage of some thousands of miles. We moved slowly out of our mooring place, waving to the faces who had become familiar to us, particularly Bernard Hill and Don McClachlan, wishing (in my case) that such loyal and powerful support were still with me, but knowing that now I had to earn some more support from other people.

This book is supposed to be a personal record, so I will abbreviate my account of our fellow passengers in Chaucerian fashion. I will not tell then that they consisted of those who were going for short-stay periods (i.e. they were returning to Cape Town on *Agulhas*); those who knew that they were going for long stays on either Gough or Tristan (i.e. they knew they were going to be on a station for a year or eighteen months) and us, (we who, despite the warnings of Peter Day and his acolytes still had no idea whether we would inhabit our proposed dwelling-place at all, or

for three weeks, six weeks, three months - or six months!)
Basically we found that we had more contact with the (few)
passengers who were going to Tristan than with those going to
Gough, exception made of the four ornithologists of Cape Town
University who were going to Gough for three weeks and of whom
more anon. The Gough meteorologists were going to be stationed
in an all-male environment for a year and their minds were
naturally set on coming to grips with that problem. So why should
they bother with other males with whom they would be acquainted
for a maximum of several days? The Gough PWD men who were
coming back on the *Agulhas* were thinking about the vast amount
of work they had to accomplish in a short space of time and though
we had several convivial hours in their company there was little
real contact. In fact, neither Nick nor I were particularly sociable
because we spent a great deal of time not only thinking about what
WE had to accomplish, but equally about how the hell we were to
accomplish it.

Even though Dr. Dave and his lovely wife were going to
Tristan for a three year period, we saw little of them because they
were both seasick for a greater part of the voyage, and as several
other passengers were similarly indisposed, we found that our
main support rested in Brendan Halpin, who knew nothing of
Tristan but had a wide experience in most of the rest of the world,
and Don Binedell of Tristan Investments, who knew a great deal
about Tristan and may well have known a great deal about other
parts of the world. As Brendan and Don were sharing a cabin,
Nick and I found it very convenient to pick their brains ensemble
and they were hospitable enough to make us welcome on several
occasions.

The first problem that had confronted me on going aboard the
Agulhas was the cabin allocation, a problem which had to be
solved almost instantaneously and without prior warning. The
two predominating factors were first that Nick and I had realised
that, whatever other bad impression this might cause, in the
interests of unity of leadership we two had to be in the same cabin;
the second, in Nick's view, and he knew far more about this than

I did, that it was important to split up boys who had been contemporaries in the same house at Denstone.

Captain Leith had awarded us four cabins, only one of which did not have port holes, the other three being consecutive on the starboard side, each having four bunks. My immediate decision was to nominate the interior cabin as the storeroom for our voluminous personal luggage (which had increased considerably during our stay in Cape Town) and to share out the remaining three among the ten customers. Nick and I asked Dick Holt to come in with us, particularly as he was to act as Nick's assistant in the postmaster job on Inaccessible. As Clive and Joe already looked like a team we put David Briggs in with them, which left a foursome of Mike Fraser and Richard Preece as senior members combined with Ian and David Gilfillan as younger ones in the remaining cabin. The results in last case were so chaotic that I hardly dared look in towards the end of the voyage and it was just lucky that Captain Leith never passed that way. The disposal of our main baggage in the interior cabin left everybody some space in their sleeping accommodation, and once we had been sailing for some thirty-six hours, we three at least had little difficulty in finding a modus vivendi which suited our various needs.

The *Agulhas* is a very modern, comfortable ship, admirably converted for the various roles she has to perform. Apart from her ice-breaker role in the Antarctic and her capacity to carry two large helicopters, her four-berth cabins each with their accompanying shower/washroom are very well appointed, as are her three laboratories (to which we, unfortunately, as a 'non-scientific' Expedition, were not admitted) and her laundry, hospital, shop and bar. During that first night the efficiency of her stabilisers became obvious because we passed through some very heavy seas without undue material damage in the cabins, even though most of the passengers were prostrated for a full twenty-four hours. Though not seasick I was awake for about half of the night and when I slept I dreamed, not nightmares but certainly not dreams of the variety where, on waking, I cried to dream again.

In a summer holiday of the mid-sixties I had engaged in a

hitch-hiking tour of Corsica, accompanied by my wife and brother-in-law, equipped with sleeping bags but without any other kind of protection. I must have had strange forebodings during the night crossing from Marseille to Ajaccio because when I dozed off in a very uncomfortable deck-chair, I suddenly had a vision of our ship passing very close to a towering cliff. The sea was not dangerous but there was some swell and the sheer proximity of the cliff was menacing: for some reason it occurred to me that Napoleon in the same circumstances would have been as powerless as I was to control his own destiny. We slipped beside the overhanging precipices for aeons of dream-time, the ship hardly swaying as silently I looked helplessly at the wave crests on my right and the huge walls of stone on my left.

It was an image which I could not shake from my mind because it recurred three times during the voyage of the 'Agulhas,' always on rough nights, having been entirely absent in the previous eighteen years. If it achieved some kind of 'realisation' I suppose that I recognised something on the one clear night when we were lying off Gough and, two months later, when the *Tristania II* spent a night off Tom's beach on Inaccessible, the scene from our cabin porthole looked astonishingly familiar: again I thought of the lonely prisoner two and a half thousand kilometres to the north whose presence a hundred and sixty years before had brought the Tristan community into being.

I spent a great deal of the voyage bird-watching from the helicopter deck (as described in Chapter 7) but even this activity did little to give me an appetite for the enormous meals available three times a day on the *Agulhas*. Breakfast at seven-thirty always consisted of five courses, and if I managed to cope with one, it meant that I was usually floored by lunch, which started at eleven-thirty. If I restricted myself to coffee at breakfast (which was, as I thought then, bad training for the rigours of Inaccessible) and then had two courses of the five-course lunch, I was immediately defeated by the five-course dinner which started at five-thirty. The other members of the Expedition, even those who suffered from seasickness, had no such inhibitions and sailed happily through three five-course meals a day. I was at a loss whether to be relieved that they were stocking up on surplus fat or to worry whether they would survive the deficiencies of the Inaccessible regime, but eventually plumped for the former attitude on the well-known 'Sufficient unto the day' maxim.

Captain Leith addressed all the passengers on the first morning, repeating almost exactly the rules which he had already laid down to us on our visit on Monday the 4th, but adding the odd piquant detail. The rules of the sea dictated that there should always be two people on the bridge, on watch. His crew were too few in number and too specialised to cover this requirement usefully and therefore the Captain proposed to put up a rota for volunteers among the passengers to fill in their names as watch-keepers during the next ten days. Once the rota was full, the ship's bar would open at lunch-time - not, he emphasised, bribery; merely coercion. He then instructed us in the art of taking a 'sea-shower,' the purpose of which was to conserve fresh water, and passed on to deal with passengers' relations with his crew. I have forgotten what retribution was promised to anybody offering alcohol to any of his sailors. I am certain it wasn't keel-hauling, and fell just short of being clapped in irons for the rest of the voyage, but only just. I remember leaving the assembly, slightly bemused, to be met by the steward who asked "Do you know which is Mr. Woolley?" I told him who I was and was immediately told that my presence was requested in the Captain's cabin at 8 pm that evening, and was somewhat reassured when told that this was a social event.

The seas had calmed down a little by the afternoon which I spent innocuously reading *Le Rouge et Le Noir*, the extra effort of reading French making it more difficult for my mind to wander. I was interested to discover when the bar opened at five-o'clock that Brendan Halpin's choice of shipboard reading was *War and Peace* and I remember telling him that in normal circumstances I would have brought at least one novel by Dostoevsky but that in the present ones I feared it might have been a trifle too depressing ...

Brendan, Don Binedell and leader of the Gough PWD team

were the other guests of Captain Leith that evening. High up in the super-structure, the roll of the ship was more exaggerated and I sat nursing a generous whisky and listening to talk of some game preservation in Africa and the Antarctic, as the Captain and Brendan swapped anecdotes. I had an interesting insight into the Captain's character when he expressed his views of certain zoologists whom he had transported to the Antarctic: their killing of Ross seals in the interest of scientific research had been clearly too much for this hard-bitten sailor. The sea was still relatively heavy and it emerged that we might be late arriving at Gough but I gleaned little else to report to Nick when I and the other guests retired at a relatively respectable hour. Nevertheless, as Dick was soundly asleep under the influence of his anti-seasickness tablets, our conversation developed into a wide-ranging discussion of our options, based on our still inadequate knowledge of the possibilities before us. The one thing which seemed certain was that some members would have to return on the *Agulhas* in only three weeks time.

Our ignorance of the possibilities was illustrated the following morning when, having risen for a early bird-watch, Nick and I repaired to the galley at 7.30 for breakfast, only to find that it was 6.30 because we had passed through a time zone overnight, a change of which our gallant captain had given us no warning whatsoever. We took refuge in the saloon where we sat sipping coffee and I reflected that exactly a week previously I had been swearing at my eldest for making me late for the train at Scarborough station. I spent the morning familiarising myself with multifarious lists, checking that all our Cape Town requisitions were in the store-room, where they were supposed to be, and that I could distinguish them from the baggage of other passengers. The lunch-time sauerkraut was really excellent and I ate large quantities but it was not a success among the younger generation and, with amazing fatuity, I made a note to keep things fairly simple once we landed on Inaccessible!

At midday I reported to the bridge for the afternoon watch, complete with heavy anorak and fully equipped to deal with anything the Cruel Sea could dish out. I was met by a blast of warmth as I stepped into the air-conditioned room and spent the next twenty minutes gradually divesting myself of various outer garments. Some three and a half hours more of 'le vaisseau glissant sur les gouffres amers' convinced me that one piece of ocean was very much like another but I had learnt something about the complexity and modernity of the machinery and equipment on the *Agulhas*; I had also learnt that the ETA at Gough was noon the following Monday. I sat down to dinner with Nick and Richard Preece.

"How did it go?" asked Nick.

"There's no need to wear warm clothes or wellingtons. It's warmer up there than it is down here and it's a damn sight more comfortable for bird-watching than the helideck."

"Who was the officer on the watch?"

"The second officer but the Captain was marching up and down behind our backs for about an hour."

"Did he know you were bird-watching?"

"You're supposed to keep the glasses on anything which moves. The only thing I saw moving were birds. Incidentally I saw a couple of Phalarope."

"What?" asked Richard.

"Phalarope. I suppose they must have been Grey Phalarope but I'll have to ask Mike."

I turned to Nick, not having seen him since breakfast.

"I spent the morning checking the stuff from Cape Town in the store-room. The only things which seem to be missing are the inflammable chemicals from the UCT but I suppose .."

Richard interrupted:

"Don't worry about those. The ornithologists from UCT gave them to me and I've tucked them up in the bunks in the spare cabin."

Suddenly I felt less hungry.

"Didn't you hear what Captain Leith said about inflammable cargo in the cabins?" I demanded.

"No, did he say anything special?"

I beat a hurried retreat and spent the next two hours repacking the bottles into two cardboard boxes, using about three rolls of lavatory paper as wadding. The ship's doctor then kindly took them in charge and stowed them in the hospital, where I couldn't resist asking him if he hadn't got a pill which could put somebody out completely till the end of the voyage. He looked at me in surprise and asked me if I was suffering that badly and I told him that I wasn't thinking about myself.

As the voyage progressed, the sea grew calmer and the *Agulhas* increased speed. By lunch-time on Saturday 9 October, Nick, who had done the 8 am to midday watch, returned with the news that we were now expected to land off Gough at 8 am on Monday. If the calmness of the sea was phenomenal, the other two phenomena which became manifest to Nick and to me over those first five days concerned, on the one hand, the attitude of everybody on the ship (apart from our members) towards us, and on the other, the attitude of our own members. Long periods of comparative comfort with not enough to do lead people to reflect and to gossip and I think that it was on that same Saturday that the two of us realised that the people who were nudging each other and pointing at us behind our backs as we moved around the ship were saying: "Those are the madmen who want to explore Inaccessible Island with a party of schoolboys." Of course, the party of schoolboys had been chewing over the vexed question of our return journey (they were all blithely assuming that there would be no problem about our landing, even though we had kept them fully informed of everything we had been told). Thus it was that David Briggs arrived in my cabin one evening when Nick and Dick were absent as an emissary from the others to find out how many people would be going home on the *Agulhas* and who they would be!

David was a good listener and a good learner and I think he quickly appreciated that neither Nick nor I had any desire to send anybody home early and I think he was reassured when I told him that if anybody had to go, I would put myself, as a non-scientist, at the head of the list. The young men who had been preparing for the Expedition for so long, who had all taken a year off in order to participate, clearly felt that they were now being subjected to an extra and unfair selection process - there was little that I could do to reassure them at that stage, particularly as we had not yet met either the Administrator of Tristan, nor the Chief Islander, who were awaiting us on Gough and on whose attitude to the Expedition so much depended.

The sea continued calm and by Sunday 10 October, my diary was recording Don Binedell as saying that he had never known it like this in his twenty years experience, though the helicopter pilots were convinced that this was only the calm before the storm. By then I had finished *Le Rouge et Le Noir* and had dug out some Schnabel recordings of Beethoven sonatas which Sylvie had given me as a parting gift. I hesitated to play them at first but was delighted when both Dick, who was a considerable musician, and Nick expressed pleasure at hearing them, even with my very poor reproduction on the old cassette recorder, which seemed to use up batteries at an inordinate speed.

That was the day when, following a service in the galley in the evening, Nick and I were invited to Captain Leith's cabin again, this time with the helicopter pilots. We were given the usual gargantuan drinks and were able to listen to the BBC World Service for about ten minutes, though I cannot recollect a single item of news. We gathered that there was little likelihood of good weather the following day but the ensuing conversation emboldened me to ask if there were any chance that some of our party might land on Gough in the course of the unloading process, particularly as there were some pollen traps which our botanist (Nick) was anxious to check on behalf of a previous visiting botanist. If we were immediately crushed by the rather unanimous negative responses from both the Captain and the pilots, which extended to the general impossibility of our landing on either Gough or Tristan, we realised some hours later that there had been no mention of the impossibility of landing on our own particular objective .....

Whether by luck or judgment, the conversation passed to other topics. It appeared that there had been some requests for more regular visits by the *Agulhas* to the island of Bouvetoya, well into the 'Roaring Fifties,' which would involve the landing of scientists, and Captain Leith was clearly perturbed by the authorities' ignorance of the implications of the request. If we passengers had been impressed by the 19 degrees of roll recorded during the first thirty-six hours on board, what would other passengers make of the 41 degrees recorded on a previous visit to the Antarctic, and how was he to cope with the perils of lying off an island in largely uncharted waters with a very recent record of undersea volcanic activity, while waiting for the odd fine day to land his scientists and another equally odd one to take them off? The Captain was clearly engrossed by his own scientific and surveying programme and was only too anxious to dispose of all his passengers in order to get on with it: we were only to discover which passengers he was most anxious to get rid of, and which kind of scientists he was most unwilling to have to take to Bouvetoya as a result of my quoting a remark by one of the ornithologists from UCT - I had better call him 'Hennessy' - about the special opportunities for ornithological research on Bouvetoya, particularly into the breeding cycle of the Pintado Petrel.

The Captain stiffened and glared.

"I suppose it was Hennessy who said that," he snapped.

"Yes, as a matter of fact, it was," I replied.

"I know Hennessy too well - this is the fourth time I have had to endure him and his fellow ornithologists on my ship."

Captain Leith lay back in his chair and gazed at the ceiling.

"You know, gentlemen," he was addressing us all - "I get very strict instructions from my Government and from their scientists about how I am to dispose of waste food during a voyage. My cooks are not allowed to throw anything overboard at dawn or at dusk, or indeed at any regular time of day, because this might interrupt the regular feeding patterns of the species which their ornithologists" (he put real venom into the ultimate noun) "are studying."

He paused.

"I obey their instructions to the letter but I also record the fact that fifty per cent of the time when my cooks are NOT throwing waste food into the ocean, there are NO ornithologists on the watch, so I send in a record of their attendance/presences to their own chief in Cape Town."

"You don't like ornithologists, Captain?" said Nick.

It was more of a remark than a question.

"I wish I was an ornithologist ... It must be rather like getting paid for testing feather-beds ..."

There was another pause, then, thoughtfully,

" ... or French letters!"

Neither Nick nor I had the wit nor the nerve to ask him how he knew, and one of the helicopter pilots asked us why we thought the ornithological part of our own programme was so important. We lapsed into Darwinism and the conversation became more general before reverting to the topic which was on all our minds, namely the weather prospects for the following day.

The Captain smiled.

"Would it interest you gentlemen to know that three-quarters of my crew are praying for bad weather tomorrow? All they want is for me to disengage the screw so that they can fish from the poop-deck. Incidentally," he turned to me, "have your members bought fishing-licences so that they can join in?"

I explained that as the Expedition only owned two fishing-lines, I had done a deal with the steward by which the Expedition had bought a group-licence for the price of two individual permits. The Captain in turn explained that the only reason he charged for the right to fish was that the fishermen made such a mess on the poop-deck that he had to pay a member of his crew extra to clean it twice a day whenever fishing was in progress. When I told them about the cost of a Day's trout fishing on a lake near my home, I soon found myself describing the techniques of netting sea-trout and salmon off the North Yorkshire coast and they, in turn, responded with descriptions of fishing in South Africa's rivers. From there, with further encouragement from Captain Leith's bottles, we moved on to shooting world-wide, and much later, back in our cabin, I seem to recollect assuring Nick that even if I had shot very many rabbits, some few grouse and the odd hare, I had never shot a flower ....

We had set Nick's alarm for 5.45 the following morning but when we got on deck at about 6 am, the pilots' forecast was proved correct as we were greeted by fog, rain and considerable swell. Visibility was down to about a quarter of a mile but breakfast was unexpectedly brought forward to 7 am and about half an hour later we were huddled on the port side, staring fixedly over the bows for a first glimpse of Gough. At about twenty past eight, an embarrassed emissary crossed the fifteen yards of intervening deck to inform us that Gough had been visible on the starboard side for the previous half hour. By then we were running down the Eastern side of that gaunt, gloomy stone fortress, the vast majority of its mountainous peaks hidden by fog and cloud. We glimpsed the Meteorological Station, a couple of hundred of feet up the sheer cliff, before heaving-to off 'The Glen,' the only safe anchorage, in a position about half a mile away from the Tristan Investments fishing boat, *Tristania II*, then hauling traps off Archway Rock. By 11.15 am attempts to fly the helicopter had been abandoned until 3 pm and at midday the Captain announced over the intercom that the screw was now disengaged and that fishing could commence on the poop-deck. The resulting exodus from the galley was the nearest thing to a stampede that I ever observed on the *Agulhas*, leaving me sipping coffee alone with Brendan and Don and observing sadly that such behaviour was very different from the life of our own dear Queen, but that if only I could etc ...

Luckily I couldn't, because such entanglements occurred that by about 2 pm our own fishing team had retired to their cabin to reorganise their tackle and their strategy. About half an hour later I was summoned to the bridge where I was informed that *Tristania II* would be in contact with 'Red Robin Bay' at 6.45 that evening and were there any messages that we would like passed?

There are in my view only two heroes in this book: they are both called Peter and neither of them figured at all in any of the initial planning of the Expedition. My friend, Major Peter

Walker, who lives about a mile away from me across Robin Hoods Bay, had retired after a distinguished teaching career some five years previously, and had then helped me with some A-level physics pupils on a part-time basis. A ham radio enthusiast with a powerful transceiver, he had immediately volunteered his services as 'lines of communication' when he heard about my impending departure, though it appeared at that stage that Denstone had its own communications network. The presence of that other enthusiastic 'ham,' Captain Peter Warren of the *Tristania II*, was a source of reassurance to us all, not only on 11 October but from then onwards and particularly in the period when he was fishing off Inaccessible in late November.

Knowing nothing about the rules of ham radio operating, an ignorance shared by all the other Expedition members, I worked out with them a kind of telegram, which we hoped when transmitted from me to Peter to Peter to Sylvie and thence to Mike at Denstone would make our continuing predicament clear. I returned to the bridge and proceeded to transmit this to Peter Warren loud and clear over the *Agulhas* transceiver across the intervening half-mile of choppy Atlantic, a transmission which must have given secret amusement to Captain Leith and his merry men, all of them no doubt aware of ham radio regulations. They must have been wondering how Peter Warren was going to rephrase our telegraphese into suitably conversational chat but to give that hero his due, he promised to relay our communication without a second's demur and to recall the *Agulhas* if 'Red Robin Bay' had anything interesting to tell us. Though I have never found anything particularly remarkable about dialling eleven digits in Yorkshire in order to talk to my brother in Hong Kong, I never ceased to marvel at the ease with which the two Peters communicated across half the world, though I suppose that as Peter Walker was part of my own little world, I had a special interest. Even though there was absolutely nothing I could do if anything were to go wrong at home, it was enormously cheering to hear that all was well, even at third or fourth hand.

They did not give up hope of trying to fly the helicopter until

6.30 pm, by which time all four varieties of the commonest South Atlantic seaboard fish had been landed: bony red Soldier-fish or Bevas, Five-fingers of various sizes, a couple of sinister- looking Snoek and three or four large Blue-fish. The most that could be said of our own efforts was that we were gaining in experience and that at least we had caught some Bevas, which were useful for bait.

The following day was fine and the helicopter started landing cargo and personnel at 8.20 am, maintaining a regular shuttle between ship and shore for most of the day. By 11.30 am, the Administrator of Tristan, Colin Redston, together with the Chief Islander, Albert Glass, had come aboard, and I made their acquaintance in the Chief Engineer's cabin, where the atmosphere exuded so much bonhomie that it was a relief when Colin quietly asked me if Nick and I would come to his cabin during the afternoon so that we might talk seriously about the Expedition's needs and its chances of fulfilling its programme.

The next encounter we had was with the ship's steward bearing considerable quantities of liquid refreshment in the direction of the Administrator's cabin outside bar hours and we realised that Colin had powers, diplomatic or otherwise, which we either lacked or had not yet had the wit to develop. Colin looked rather like the archetypal colonial civil servant of thirty years previously - in fact, rather like my father (when Chief Commissioner of the Gold Coast) looked at that time: short clean-shaven apart from moustaches, tanned complexion, affable and apparently easy going though we had already realised that Colin was not altogether satisfied with some aspects of the way in which we had been landed/ foisted on him. Nevertheless I had realised that here was somebody to whom I could talk and be sure that I would have a sympathetic audience - he was no more the colonial 'Blimp' than my father had been and he had the same concern for and knowledge of the peoples for whom he was responsible. I was therefore slightly upset when Nick turned up in our cabin some ten minutes after the appointed time - I can't remember the reason but it was with some asperity that I reminded him that it was time to go. We went, and talked for some two hours, at least one of which was devoted to the sempiternal topic of getting on and off Inaccessible. The other hour was actually much more useful because it covered practical things like supplies, hire of boat(s), the purchase of stamps for our Post Office, the character of our Tristan guides and the likelihood of fresh water being available at the various choices for our hut-site on the island.

The last subject was dissected in no uncertain fashion by Albert, whose argument could be summarised in about three simple sentences.

"Even though the most accessible and best protected landing-site is Waterfall, the way up to the plateau from there is now almost unscalable, except to an experienced mountaineer. There is not enough water on the plateau to keep you all supplied, even if by some chance you could manage to persuade Captain Leith and his pilots to land you there. The only feasible landing site is Blenden Hall, where there are plentiful supplies of superb water, which offers a reasonable route to the plateau, and where Nelson and Andrew, the guides I have chosen for you, can probably find a site for your hut which will give enough protection from the prevailing wind."

If there is the odd uncharitable comment about Albert's reliability elsewhere in this narrative, particularly in the Cooking chapter (7), let me record now how accurate was his judgment in this vital matter and how his guidance helped to promote the eventual complete success of the Expedition. He was equally accurate about our guides:

"You may think that Nelson is too old because he is over sixty-five. He knows Inaccessible better than anybody and he is so fit that he should be able to walk you off your feet, as should Andrew, my cousin, who is ten years younger than Nelson but who also knows Inaccessible well."

It was proved to us only too often that they could both walk us off our feet and Andrew proved as reliable a guide as Nelson, even though we learnt later that his knowledge of Inaccessible prior to landing approximated to our own ....

That was the day when we began to feel the monotony of the voyage and we were grateful when some of the junior officers organised visits to the engine-room for two of our members at a time. Once the helicopter had carried out its quota of flying-hours for the day, the screw had disengaged and frantic fishing began again. There was some excitement when the Radio Officer landed a gigantic Blue-fish (about 2m x ½m) and our own efforts were crowned with more success in that one of us landed a smaller one. Nevertheless by the following day, the 13 October, the entry in my diary reads as follows:

'A cold gusty morning which seemed to prohibit flying, certainly until the afternoon. We have been on *Agulhas* for a week now and there are long periods when we have absolutely nothing to do except wait for the bar to open or the next meal. Two weeks ago I was teaching 5b *Romeo and Juliet*: now I am looking out on to a grey ocean with the odd Giant Petrel or Great Skua flying across and wondering what the hell I am doing here?

'A thoroughly boring day; the helicopter only made one or two flights and the ground staff had real trouble securing it when it came back (the pilots jumped for their lives and let them get on with it!) Then the ship sailed off to find a flat piece of ocean floor at two hundred metres depth so that a visiting scientist could drop a gauge to measure the tide flow - they found one but they could not drop the gauge because the wind was gusting to eighty knots.

'No cargo landed at all. Crayfish for dinner. Somebody nearly caught a five-foot shark, but it slipped off the gaff.'

We were still agonising about our transport problems and it was on this day that Nick came up with the idea that we should all stay on Inaccessible until December, when half the Expedition who had obligations at home should return to Cape Town on *Tristania II*, while the other half should remain on Tristan working for their keep until the Royal Navy appeared. We put the idea to Colin Redston, who promised to think about it overnight. Even though he rejected it the following morning because his islanders were already underemployed and our people would have been depriving them of work, in the event, our proposal, though not in the proportions to our original suggestion, was very much what occurred. The majority of the Expedition, who were only taken off Inaccessible just before Christmas, was obliged to remain on Tristan for nearly five weeks because of inclement(!) weather and only finally got back to Inaccessible for a last three weeks (together with Mike Swales and two new members who had all made the long journey out via Cape Town and 'Tristania II') before the Royal Navy arrived. As this is written with the benefit of hindsight, it is difficult to convey our sense of depression when Colin very sensibly told us why our suggestion was a non-starter, but our depression on that particular day was mitigated by the fact that the weather was fine and things were happening.

We were learning to appreciate that in the South Atlantic, when things happen, they happen fast. It was a glorious fine morning and the first one (if not the only one) when we could see the high peaks of Gough. The helicopter was already at work by eight o'clock, and we were soon checking our own cargo in the hold, putting all containers likely to be affected by the weather in enormous black plastic bags, then assembling helicopter loads in their rope nets. It was at some point in the checking of roof-trusses when I foolishly attempted to lift a pile of six without anybody to help and felt a familiar twinge in my lower spine, that my morale slumped. It slumped still further when, at about half-past ten, two of the UCT ornithologists came back from Gough in order to help the *Agulhas* crew distinguish between which was their cargo and which was ours but we had little time to worry about the implications because it soon became clear that the unloading would be completed by about 1 pm.

Nick and Mike went off for a helicopter tour of Gough which gave them a chance to take some photographs even though they did not have a chance to land. Following a further talk with Colin that evening, we held an Expedition meeting which went rather better than the one in Cape Town, probably because everybody had appreciated how much our fate still hung in the twin balances of the weather and Captain Leith's goodwill: furthermore the problem of landing ON Inaccessible rather obscured the problems of how everybody was to stay on and come off at the appropriate time. When Nick went off to keep watch on the bridge, I was invited to the helicopter pilots' cabin, where I quickly realised that personally, they were both keen to say that they had been the first to land on Inaccessible Island. I was also cheered to learn that the helicopter could easily accommodate all our members in one flight - it could, in fact, accommodate eighteen, which, momentarily, made me wonder why only two of our team had been allowed to tour Gough from the air: it was not the 'eggs in one basket' syndrome which applied so much as the 'eggs in one unauthorised basket.'

That night we sailed the two hundred and thirty miles northwards to Tristan, which, coincidentally, was expecting the visit of a Scandinavian liner at the same time as our arrival. Knowing this, we had spent some of the previous twenty-four hours writing extra letters because the liner was en route to Cape Town. By mid-morning both ships were lying off the settlement of Edinburgh but the conditions were far too rough for the helicopter to fly or for boats to get out of the harbour and even this is written with the benefit of hindsight - we saw nothing: the liner continued its voyage without a backward glance or our letters - I don't know if the Captain of that liner realised what concentrated hatred his departure aroused - even now, two years later, I hope he's suffering somewhere, whether in this life or the next. We adjourned to the galley for lunch where, since the departure of the majority of our passengers to Gough, waiter service had supplanted the cafeteria system.

I was sitting next to Richard Preece and became somewhat irritated when he asked me to repeat something for the third time.

"Good God, Richard, are you deaf?" I asked, and was mortified and humiliated to get the answer (in the mildest of tones),

"Yes, I am, rather."

This exchange gave unnecessary amusement to Nick, who later recounted to me an incident earlier in the voyage when the Captain's voice had been heard over the intercom saying:

"Doctor, please come to the bridge," and two minutes later

47

our Doctor Preece had presented himself there. with some consequential confusion ....

By one o'clock the Captain had grown impatient: the *Agulhas* was heading for Inaccessible because conditions were so impossible at Tristan and we learnt (from Colin!) that there was some possibility of our being landed by pontoon (rubber barges) that afternoon, minus our guides and our supplies from Tristan. As we had previously realised that if we and our eight tonnes of cargo were once landed on Tristan, there was no way that we would then be able to transport the cargo (particularly the sections of the hut) across the intervening twenty-two miles of sea by means of the Tristan barge, we greeted the news with somewhat mixed feelings. At about three o'clock Nick and I were summoned to the bridge where we were joined by Albert Glass. who pointed out the deficiencies of Waterfall Beach as a landing site. Its advantage was that it was on the leeward side of the Island - it was one of the regular anchorages for the Tristan Investments fishing boats when they were operating off Inaccessible: it also was assured of fresh water. Its disadvantages from our point of view were that the beach was a very small one which offered no access in either direction to other beaches without a boat and a lot of calm weather; the precipice behind was possibly scaleable by experienced climbers who might teach our young men if given enough time ....

I looked at the cliff through glasses and quickly discounted my own chances of ever seeing the top of the island if we were to land at its foot. As a result of our representations we had superb views of the cliffs as the ship began to circumnavigate the island in an anti-clockwise direction. though we were plunging heavily in the swell. We hove to off a triangular promontory of low-lying land which Albert identified as Blenden Hall (the *Blenden Hall* was a ship which was wrecked there in 1821. from which wreck not only did most of the crew and passengers survive and live off fish, seabirds and penguins for several weeks. but also managed to construct a raft and get across to Tristan to make their plight known). Albert pointed out the 'gentle' ascent to the top of the plateau and the sources of fresh water on the beach [*See Plate 2*].

Captain Leith was watching the breakers and he summoned us to his side.

"If I land you by pontoon now, gentlemen," he observed, "you will lose about thirty per cent of your cargo in that swell."

Without looking at Nick, and taking a deep breath, I answered that in those circumstances we would prefer not to be landed on this particular occasion. I was taking some kind of risk because I knew we might be blowing all chances of landing anywhere; on the other hand I knew Captain Leith was quite anxious to get rid of us and that Colin would be more than embarrassed to have us dumped on him at Tristan with no chance of our getting our cumbersome woodframes across to Inaccessible on his frail barge(s) and only a 50/50 chance that *Agulhas* might condescend to perform the operation on her return in three weeks time ....

There was a moment's silence as everybody took in the full import; then the Captain gave the order to continue the circumnavigation. We anchored about half a mile offshore in Carlisle Bay (the lee side) and fishing promptly commenced on the poop-deck. Later we learnt that we were due back at Tristan at eight o'clock the following morning and were able to meditate on the thought-provoking catch of a baby shark within an hour of the beginning of the piscatorial activities.

Shingle, tussock, hut and "gentle" ascent.

Approaching Inaccessible

Expedition Map of Inaccessible

Nelson and Andrew with their baulk of timber.

Invertebrate Zoologist playing in the Skua Bog.

CHAPTER 4

' .... GONE.'

quando n'apparve una montagna bruna
per la distanza, e parvemi alta tanto,
quanto veduta non n'aveva alcuna.

When at last hove up a mountain, grey
With distance, and so lofty and so steep,
I had never seen the like on any day.
Dante: Inferno XXVI

He had forty-two boxes, all carefully packed,
With his name painted clearly on each:
But, since he omitted to mention the fact,
They were all left behind on the beach.
Lewis Carroll: The Hunting of the Snark

The 16 October was another of those days which proved my theory expressed in the previous chapter that there are only two tempi of life in the South Atlantic: dead slow and full speed ahead. The weather was still rough but visibility had improved considerably and though the peak of Tristan was still swathed in cloud, its grey cliffs loomed over us as we ran down the north-west side early in the morning [*See Plate 3*]. Soon after eight o'clock the helicopter went off on a trial flight and when, with Agulhas bow-thrusters hard at work to level the ship, it re-landed, the Tristan passengers were immediately given instructions to prepare for landing. So quickly did they prepare that Brendan Halpin neglected to remind anybody about his heavy luggage in the hold, an omission which was eventually to leave him without any of his equipment for the three weeks he was on Tristan! When the Captain let us know that there would be transport for two of us to visit Tristan at about eleven o'clock on what might be described as a social visit, we had already decided that I would be going.

accompanied by David Briggs to represent the younger generation. We knew that Pat, the postman, would be coming out on a return helicopter flight bearing all the stamps (they were to be cancelled by the unique 'Inaccessible Island Post Office' cachet which the GPO had granted us before our departure) which we had ordered by radio while lying off Gough, which meant that Nick and Dick would have to be on board to greet him. The other determining factor in my own case was that we had learnt that Mrs. Redston, the Administrator's wife, was French, and in David's, his ability to make an immediate good impression. It would be disingenuous not to admit that both Nick and I realised that what we were undertaking was very much a public relations exercise, the success of which was essential for the well-being of the Expedition if and when we landed on Inaccessible.

I have regarded helicopter travel as a necessary evil ever since my days in the Army and nothing in the ensuing flight did anything to make me think that it had improved as a mode of transport in the intervening twenty-five years. The strength of the wind against us was considerable and our progress to the settlement bore some resemblance to that of an aerial crab but my faith in the skill of our pilots was confirmed as they landed us in front of the Residency on the field which serves as Tristan's airport. Leading the large group who met us were Colin and Albert with several passengers from the *Agulhas* to whom we had bidden a fond farewell the night before. We were introduced to a succession of people, in particular the two expatriate schoolmasters, John Cooper and Richard Grundy; then Albert went off with the helicopter pilots and Colin took us to the Residency to meet his wife and two small sons.

It is difficult to convey the overwhelming friendliness of atmosphere in which David and I floated during those three hours that we spent on Tristan. Marie-José Redston was preparing a lunch for about twenty people and I chatted to her in the kitchen as a succession of expatriate wives and island ladies passed backwards and forwards with contributions to the meal, plates, cutlery and glasses, occasionally interrupting our conversation to ask for instructions, which Marie-José seemed to improvise in a fashion so familiar to me that for a moment I thought I was at home. I had to make a conscious effort to wrench my mind back to the number of things that I had to remember to ask, but Colin helped by appearing at my elbow to remind me that we were due to visit Albert prior to lunch. We collected David from the main lounge, whose window encompassed an enormous view of the empty Atlantic (*Agulhas* was sheltering from the wind somewhere round the east side), wherein he had been explaining the objectives of the Expedition to a largely unfamiliar expatriate audience, though Brendan was in the background giving unobtrusive help.

We set out on concrete pathways which suddenly became narrow cinder tracks, flanked by New Zealand flax with its brown purple buds which towered above our heads; we emerged into open grassy spaces with outcrops of volcanic rock and piles of volcanic rubble lying about. I was busily talking to Colin about the Expedition's needs when David jogged my elbow to remind me of the needs of those members not fortunate enough to be with us. As far as I can recollect, I threw my camera at him with instructions to 'take pictures,' and 'pick up some bits of rock:' he accomplished both exercises with distinction. We made our way between the single storey houses, each with its walled garden, until we emerged before a particularly large building, apparently of breeze-block construction fronted by a large grassy area with a flagstaff - a sight which reminded me very forcibly of my Senior District Commissioner father's bungalow in Kibi, then part of the Gold Coast colony, when my brother and I were visiting in the early nineteen-fifties ... I was musing on this memory when David tugged my sleeve and we stopped while he took a picture of the volcanic eruption of 1961, eastward of the big building (which turned out to be Prince Philip Hall) because, David said, "I want to get the steam coming out of the top."

The news that the eruption of 1961 was still emitting steam almost gave me a heart attack but nobody else seemed to be showing any concern so I restrained the expression of my desire to be re-transported to the *Agulhas* forthwith.

We arrived at Albert's house and were served with large drinks in an entirely male environment, typical of Tristan but one to which I had difficulties in adjusting at that point, despite our ten days on the *Agulhas*. At an appropriate pause in the conversation with the helicopter pilots, I managed to pass Albert all the members' passports with a request that they be suitably stamped with a record of our sojourn in his territory. I then passed on to a rapid gabble about our need for dinghies, potatoes, onions, ovens, two-way radios and other minor necessities. I was reassured by both Albert and the pilots: the former told me that our guides were all ready to go, plus potatoes, and that anything which was not transported by helicopter would inevitably arrive by barge within eight or ten days; the latter pair made it evident to me that there was a strong possibility of our being landed on Inaccessible later that day if the weather conditions continued as unsuitable for landing on Tristan as they then were. With these reassurances I had to be content and we made our way back to the Residency, skirting the neat walled gardens with their protective flax, David pausing to take more photographs and I mentally ticking off more items on my list. Everybody we met exchanged greetings and I quickly learnt to substitute "Hello" for my too formal "Good Morning."

Preparations for lunch in the Residency had reached such epic proportions by the time we returned that the broad table seemed to have no more room on it for food. I renewed acquaintance with Philip and Peter Redston and met Chris Jebb, the expatriate treasurer, and his wife, Maria. They in turn introduced me to other guests, some of whom I never saw again because they were due to take passage on the returning *Agulhas*, others whom I got to know very well some six weeks later. David was talking to Richard Grundy but, like me, was beginning to absorb the pilot's final instructions to us to be sure to be ready for the return flight at two o'clock. Neither of us can remember very much about our conversation during the last hour of lunch though we agreed, when we compared notes, that it was the best meal we had eaten since our departure from England. Brendan took me aside for a moment and repeated the advice which he had already given to Nick.

"Remember that there will be no time for democracy once your Expedition lands: you've got to lead it."

It was good advice and well-meant, but if my own profound ignorance of many of the requirements of the specialists, combined with Nick's inexperience in the art of making one's presence felt, occasionally led in the aftermath of the erection of the hut to several decisions of dubious democratic validity (because they were always produced and passed by the same 17% minority), this was no bad thing in establishing some sense, not of unity of purpose, which was already there anyway, but in making the non-vocal majority aware that if they had deep feelings about something, at least it could be expressed. If Brendan's advice has led to a digression at this point, it is because I still haven't forgotten it.

I think it was my anxiety about not missing the helicopter which led to our exodus when some members of the lunch-party were still busy enjoying dessert or coffee. We moved down the garden path of the Residency in stately fashion and David took a last photo of me (clean-shaven), hand in hand with a somewhat dubious Philip Redston. At the gateway to the field where the tethered helicopter awaited its pilots and passengers, we were introduced to our two guides, Nelson Green and Andrew Glass, whose luggage was so extensive even allowing for five bags of potatoes that I assumed that it included a large proportion of our requirements (excluding the boat). Both men had been involved in the evacuation and resettlement following the 1961 eruption so presumably they had travelled by helicopter before. Certainly neither showed the least concern as we sped back to the waiting *Agulhas* and settled unhesitatingly on her pocket-handkerchief deck: David and I were so full of our experiences and so agog at what was yet to come that we didn't pay much attention either. Nick was there with other members to help us unload and accompany Nelson and Andrew back to our cabin, where we ensconced them on the settee and plied them with refreshment while other members came in to meet them and make them welcome.

I got the impression that Captain Leith was not altogether pleased at our protracted lunch, even though David and I had obeyed our instructions so exactly that we had almost been guilty of rudeness in leaving our Tristan hosts too soon. *Agulhas* set off towards Inaccessible within about one minute of the final 'Helicopter Secure' announcement and about half-way over, we were told that in view of the continuing swell, it was hoped to land us by helicopter on Blenden Hall, starting at about five o'clock that evening. There ensued a gathering together of our 'personal' baggage, much of which regrettably (because of its weight), consisted of boxes from the ship's 'bond' supplies. The Captain had generously allowed us to buy as much as we wanted and though I had pointed out the weight and bulk problems involved in buying too much beer or minerals, we had allowed each member to put in his individual order to me, though we had made it clear that everybody had to pay cash on delivery. If I had had a little more foresight, it would have been so easy to put not only these boxes, but also our kit-bags and coffer-bags into one extra rope net, which would have obviated a great deal of the ensuing hassle, but as it was, we all eventually moved up to the heli-deck with about three times as much personal luggage as an individual could possibly carry at one go.

Prior to that, it had occurred to me that as the entire Expedition was to embark on the first flight and as only the two pilots would be accompanying us and then returning to pick up our cargo nets, perhaps somebody ought to know how to 'bring in' a loaded helicopter, disengage the hook and signal the 'all free.' I made my problem known to a friendly member of the deck crew who struck his forehead and cheerfully observed:

"Jesus Christ, I'd forgotten about that! Never mind. You'll have to do it and it's quite simple ..." He gave me three minutes instructions in the art, concluding with a generous warning to "for Chrissake keep clear of the rear rotor arm or it'll knock your bloody head off!" My morale thus fortified, we embarked with an additional warning to all passengers on the same subject, which I thought appropriate to repeat to Richard Preece ....

Communication between passengers in a helicopter flight is, in my view, practically impossible and communication between passenger and pilot completely so because of the latter's headphones. The pilots knew where Blenden Hall was just as Nelson knew on which area of Blenden Hall he would have liked us to be landed. We did manage to avoid landing in the middle of a rich emerald coloured field which later turned out to be that delectation of the hearts of our Invertebrate Zoologist and ornithologist, the Skua Bog, but Nelson couldn't see enough, never mind communicate it, to tell the pilots when they eventually landed very near the shoreline, that they were at the wrong end of the baseline of the Blenden Hall triangle.

We unloaded while the pilots took pictures of themselves and Nelson indicated a point somewhere in the distance where he wanted the cargo nets dropped, near the site where he thought we should build the hut. Picking up as much hand luggage as we thought we could carry, we followed him in a straggling line which rapidly began to look like a slow-motion replay of the retreat from Mons, as the hazards of the Inaccessible terrain became apparent to us. The only possible route was along the shingle because the edge of the head high tussock grass was absolutely clearly defined and there was no way we could have walked through that with our present burdens [*See Plate 2*]. We picked our way from stone to stone, ever conscious of Nick's warning about injuries, fractures and sprains and, as the walk began to protract itself, even more conscious of the weight of our luggage. Larding the lean earth, I struggled onwards in about fourth or fifth position, terribly worried lest I should not be in situ for the return of the helicopter with its first load. I think I lost more weight in that half-hour than I did in the ensuing six weeks but, at last, after passing some promising outflows of water from the tussock on to the shingle, Nelson struck up to his right into the vegetation. The only reason that I knew he had done this was because I saw the linkman, who must have been lying third or fourth a hundred yards ahead of me, do the same thing: I focused desperately on a washed-up pink plastic float somewhere near the point of exodus and having achieved that objective, I too turned smartly to my right.

Nelson had chosen his ground admirably but my admiration was strictly limited to that moment because I was struggling through uncharted tussock: I came to a halt, perspiring profusely, as the helicopter swept in. Somebody must have made signals and somebody must have disengaged that first load; I know I was there and that I was croaking instructions but my practical assistance was minimal.

By the time the second load buzzed into sight we had another two pairs of hands to receive it and I was standing in the correct position, arms upraised in a 'V,' leaning forward to counteract the draught from the blades as the helicopter closed in on me. A moment's desperate wrenching at the hook and I gave the thumbs up; then, once the machine was clear, it was a question of moving all the cargo out of the net and collecting all the hooks, ropes and nets together for return to *Agulhas* once the last load had been delivered. By the time we had done that, the chopper was in view again, this time carrying about half the sections of the hut. I guided it in, we disentangled the ropes, leaving the hut sections stacked in a neat pile, and I moved forward to choose the next site about twenty yards away, thinking to keep the loads within as small a total area as possible. Just as she homed in on me once more, the net swinging within about twenty feet of my face, as I leant forward to withstand the draught from the blades, I heard a desperate yell of fear from behind me. Turning, I saw sections of hut being blown into the air like a pack of cards, moved by the same draught. It was too late to change the site because the load was on the ground within five seconds, but luck was on our side: nobody was hit and the sections were not damaged, their fall being cushioned by the tall tussock which held them up and enabled us to find every single section in the long run.

The chopper made her final run at about ten past six and once its load was disengaged, landed on a hurriedly chosen, relatively flat area which we had already earmarked for the tents. The pilots helped us to load the nets, surveyed the terrain and told us they were sorry they had to dash but they understood that Captain Leith had a bottle of champagne waiting for them in the cooler of the *Agulhas*. They took off into the setting sun but we had no time to shed bitter tears. Nick and I were identifying and locating packages, half the remainder were hurriedly putting up tents and the other half were making another trip back to the original landing-site to bring back more 'hand' luggage. I think it was on this occasion that we became aware of David Brigg's enormous physical strength as he carried one of the hundredweight bags of potatoes the whole length of the shingle beach without stopping. At least there was no danger of anybody stealing the cargo left lying at that far end of the strand, some of which was not picked up until at least two days later.

The race to get the tents up before dark was won by a very narrow margin. How we would have managed without the loan of the two tents from Tristan with which Richard Grundy had equipped our guides I cannot imagine, as the absolute maximum which our own tents could accommodate was nine. The only way that Nick, Dick and I could fit into 'ours' was for Nick and me to crawl in first and each get as close as possible to our respective sides while Dick crawled in down the middle. (Anybody wanting to answer the call of nature in the middle of the night was distinctly unpopular).

Previously I had distributed oranges and chocolates for supper and we had put all our kit-bags and coffer-bags under a shield of black plastic coverings.

I must have slept for a least three hours altogether but the three hours were broken up into half-hour sections, partly caused by the sheer discomfort of the situation, partly by the succeeding rainstorms and probably, most of all, by the disquiet in my own mind. After the race along the shingle I was convinced that I was too old to be a useful member of the group, particularly as I was becoming only too well aware of symptoms of back-strain following our jollifications in the hold of *Agulhas*. Previous, very infrequent, occurrences of the same symptoms had taught me that a few days inactivity was a reliable cure but I hesitated to suggest such a solution to my hard-pressed co-leader who nevertheless comprehended my condition almost immediately and loyally helped me during the next two or three days.

There was no way that anybody could help anybody mentally during the course of the first night. Some were so excited simply because we had succeeded in landing that they were able to sleep, others so tired from physical exertion that they too slept. I had always revelled in the sound of rain hitting a canvas roof over my head, just as I enjoy spray hitting my face over the bows of a boat. Now, however, whenever the rain stopped, the roar of the breakers took over and I lay, tightly wedged, telling myself how lucky I was and wondering how long it would take me to find something to eat for breakfast the following morning.

*   *   *

Rain rapped on the canvas and began, spasmodically, to drip through in the odd place. We lay, fully clothed, in our sleeping bags trying not to impinge on each other's space and also to avoid touching the tent walls; for about half an hour we exchanged the odd jocularity ("God 'elp pore saylors on a nite like this"), cut off from all other human sounds despite the proximity of the other tents. By the time the first rain storm had died away, Dick, on my right, had dropped into a grateful slumber, unrocked by the treacherous swells, and if Nick, on the far side, was awake, he certainly wasn't talking. Intermittent with the surf-roar came the odd bird-call, unidentifiable, unrecognisable, plaintive, haunting ...

Mentally I damned the rain which had made it risky for me to expand six inches to my left and also risked getting under the plastic coverings over our perishable cargo.

Where did I see those boxes of Kendal Mint Cake? - they would do for breakfast if I can lay my hands on them: maybe they're in that pile uphill to the left.

Where are the cookers?

If I can find the cheese and some biscuits, that's lunch, but what about supper? Soup and stew? If we can find the cookers, the paraffin dump is straight ahead uphill, well clear of the other loads, no problem.

Why am I saying 'no problem'? That's what Mike Swales would say and we've had nothing but bloody problems and it's only sheer bloody luck that we're safely on this bloody island. Luck? What's luck got to do with it? What makes you think we're so lucky anyway? From now on we're stuck until some outside power deigns to give us assistance. We've no immediate means of communication and bugger-all transport.

What was it Major Minford used to snap at me in those precise accents which seemed to indicate intense hatred but which (I only learned too late) in fact showed his real concern for and interest in the proper education of young subalterns?

"Woolley," (or, about once every two months on the rare occasions when I happened to be in favour) "My dear John, NEVER undertake any operation unless you have previously assured yourself of the adequacy and efficiency of your communications and transport."

Never mind that. What about that other more famous military personality who observed that an army marched on its stomach? Clive certainly does.

Their stomachs are full at the moment but they'll be expecting a proper meal by tomorrow evening. Do they realise what the problems are or have they been so far indoctrinated that they can't believe that there are some? Don't be unjust, of course they can.

Ease position of the back.

What are you going to do about your back? Not much you can do except the minimum physical activity and the maximum intellectual. Intellectual! Fat lot of use that's going to be.

Don't be unfair.

"Ne sois pas injuste!"

I can hear her saying it. She'd be in her element cooking for this lot on the old camp-fire but I can't see her appreciating the sleeping space available in this tent. What time is it? Two hours difference in the UK: she'll be watching telly.

Hullo! It's raining again. Ow! Must remember to take the books out of the haversack when I make the pillow tomorrow

night. There's something flapping. Is it part of a tent or a plastic cover? I'm not moving till it stops raining ... If it stops raining ...
'Here I am a fat man in a wet tent
Being gnawed at by my doubts, damning the rain ...'

*　　　*　　　*

By quarter to six the following morning I had had enough. The last rainstorm had died away about an hour previously and I knew I had no further chance of sleep, so I extricated myself as carefully and silently as possible, leaving two semi-conscious forms behind me. Donning the boots left just inside the tent flap entrance the previous night, I squelched towards the nearest black plastic mound, identified the loose end which I had heard flapping overnight and realised thankfully that no harm had been done. Cautiously I ventured further afield, locating the various sites of dumps and burrowing industriously into any container which seemed to be of culinary interest. By the time I had found the Kendal Mint Cakes, the other tents were beginning to empty and eager hands were investigating and identifying containers. I distributed 'breakfast' and indicated the whereabouts of fresh water to those who hadn't yet noticed it.

Nelson and Andrew were already beginning to ferret about for stray containers but we had to summon them to come and give us advice about the siting of the hut, obviously the first priority if site-clearing were to begin as soon as possible.

We (Nick and I) were trying to think of about six factors: (a) fresh water supply, (b) shelter from prevailing winds, (c) firm base, (d) minimal amount of terrain to clear, (e) appropriate very proximate site for landing of helicopter and (f) ditto for siting of wind generator. We were also having to listen to the supposedly helpful but frequently inane comments of the young.

Nelson and Andrew were sensible but inarticulate so that in the end I think we chose a site about twenty yards too high, a site which necessitated rather more earth and rock clearing than we could encompass with our solitary pick ...

Once we had decided on the site, however, we were able to nominate teams to the different tasks of site-clearing, the collection and identification of cargo and the erection of the two metal-tube storage tents, which were of prime importance not only because of the need to shelter our perishable cargo, but also because we knew that if our tents should prove fallible, they would be our ultimate refuge. There was no question of our levelling a site for the latter - once the location of the hut had been decided the two nearest roughly level pieces of ground were appropriated and when, in mid-morning, the surveyor popped up with an alternative suggestion for the siting of the hut, he got a distinctly dusty reception. Despite his intervention, by lunch-time (expedited because I had found the cheese and biscuits) we had put up the frames of both storage shelters and had covered one. The shape of the far end of the eleven hundred square feet of sloping terrain which we had to flatten in order to erect the hut was beginning to emerge.

Having found one of the Valor cookers, the evening meal also went according to plan though it brought home to me once and for all the importance of bulk. The vagaries of the cooker and the gastronomic charms of Inaccessible will be recounted in Chapter 7: depressing though they were, it was the vagaries of our communications which were confirmed that afternoon as Joe failed to make radio contact with Tristan from our site position. We had made an arrangement with our Tristan friends to have a 'sched' every forty-eight hours at 4.15 pm but there was some confusion about this because Joe then made a private arrangement (or thought he did) with Andy Repetto, the Tristan radio operator, to make 'scheds' at 12.30 pm. Apart from our having to climb to the top of Inaccessible to make the 'sched,' the Tristan contact had also to make a hike of some mile and a half in order to reach a position where Inaccessible was clearly in 'line of sight,' if frequently invisible.

Apart from their tirelessness in recuperating packages and establishing centralised dumps, Nelson and Andrew played a major part in the clearing of the hut site. One of their forays down to the shore produced a couple of washed-up plastic fish boxes, together with some lengths of strong rope; a patent Inaccessible wheelless-barrow quickly evolved from this flotsam.

I suppose the next four days and nights were, strangely, the time when we were most united in our efforts. Whenever something had to be done, a pair of hands materialised to do it and even though the tents were quite astonishingly uncomfortable, by the fourth morning I was recording 'a good night's sleep.' I think everybody was so totally exhausted that we all slept: though the weather was frequently windy and overcast, the rain kept off until Wednesday the 20th and as I don't think anybody changed their clothes during the building period (though we did take our boots off before we went to bed), this was a piece of good fortune which we did not appreciate until about a fortnight later when we had experienced three days and nights of continuous strong winds and rain.

On our second full day, Nelson and Joe made the first ascent to the top of the island, Nelson picking the line of what came to be called 'West Road' through the dense tussock and up the bare steep hillside, relying infallibly on his memory of the route from some thirty years previously [See Plate 4]. Joe made radio contact with Tristan using our own walkie-talkie and I was much relieved, though I might have been less so if I had realised that we were to have no further contact with Tristan for nine days.

During that afternoon, Nick and I walked along the shingle to the west and the last of our 'hand' luggage, in this case, the two remaining boxes of alcohol (the medicinal ones) still lying where we had left them what seemed like about a year before. It wasn't easy to hold a conversation while picking our way from stone to stone with the wave-roar to our right, but we managed to exchange the odd thought, even when he treated me to an explanation of some rock which looked as if somebody had dropped a lot of scrambled egg over it and which Nick described as a pyroclastic bomb. We were both pleased to be away from the hassle for a couple of hours, listening happily to the 'cheep' of the Inaccessible Rails in the low tussock just beyond our dump-site, and returning fairly slowly with the sun on our backs and the Skuas reluctantly taking off before we walked over them.

We agreed to try and start breakfast an hour earlier the following morning in order to take more advantage of daylight. The fact that breakfast was ready at the appointed time was a source of some dismay to certain junior members but it proved profitable in the long run up to lunch because our teams were able to diversify more and were able to see more for their efforts. Ian and Dick started setting up the wind generator and David and Joe started laying the floor of the hut as the site-clearers advanced more closely to 'my' cooking and storage tents: the eventual proximity of those 'tents' to the 'kitchen' in the hut, and their service as wind buffers against the prevailing gales is something from which I still take modest satisfaction, in view of the clamour prior to their positioning. Personally I was very busy because the wind kept shifting direction which made the stove extremely temperamental, but I had managed to track down some more food supplies.

The sun shone, and during the afternoon our guides pointed out a school of whales to us. Having latched on and watched for some minutes, I then brought Richard on target and switched my attention to something else, only to hear him triumphantly yell "There she blows!" about ten seconds later, a sight which I missed out on completely.

I think this was the day when I had some desperately lonely moments simply because I was beginning to work out that the difference between me and everybody else was that the others had no family responsibilities; they had loving families but not ones where anybody was dependent on them, hence a dichotomy which I only visualised clearly some three days later. Despite our obvious progress, I don't think I was the only one to have felt doubts that evening because the doctor prescribed some medicinal alcohol for the whole party and this was a good thing in view of the weather conditions that night and next morning.

I quote from my diary for Wednesday, 20 October:

'When I got up at six it was grey and windy and the plastic

covering over the cooking hut had been blown off during the night -I managed to get it back on again after a desperate struggle and put some of the partitions of the hut against the side of the prevailing wind - this made all the difference and I managed to get two lots of porridge and the tea done by five past seven, having started cooking at half-past six. The usual potato chore while the others struggled with two final rocks in the way of the last floor section - the floor was completed at ten past twelve but it was too windy to start man-handling the wall sections so we took the afternoon off. Some of us walked along the shingle towards North Point and sat watching the penguins but rain started to fall at two o'clock which drove us back to the tents. There was a lull at four-thirty which enabled me to cook dinner and also made it possible for the rest to eat it. Another night of intermittent rain.'

The wind was gusting strongly the following morning but we decided to go ahead and erect the hut. There were several moments when every member of the Expedition apart from the man with the nuts and bolts was clinging on to different bits of wall but as the structure grew it gained in strength and by lunchtime, with half the roof on, the wind was beginning to drop. By suppertime the only things missing were the covering strips for the exterior wall joins and the interior wire stays from roof to floor.

It was much more comfortable to sleep on the floor of the hut having changed clothes but my greatest pleasure came from looking at the sea through a real window. I wondered whether my sense of loneliness was caused by the insecurity of our existence and realised with some astonishment that I had not as yet been frightened. My moments of unhappiness stemmed from the fact that I was far too used to comfort, hence my preoccupation in moments of relaxation with my personal possessions, none of which (as I rationalised it in my diary) had the slightest value, except the diary. It was going to be difficult if the kitchen cut me off as well as the age-gap but there wasn't much point in agonising: we could now carry out the 'programme' and therefore requests for help, particularly transportation, from the outside world were unlikely to be heard with anything like the sympathy which had pertained up till now.

Not having heard any music for a week, I found a Vivaldi cassette and stuck it on: I had no earphones and the others had to bear it but I had missed so much that I didn't care ...

CHAPTER 5

ENVIRONMENTAL STUDIES

Adrian: *Though this island seemed to be desert, -*
Antonio: *Ha, ha, ha!*
Sebastian: *So you're paid.*
Adrian: *Uninhabited, and almost inaccessible,*
Sebastian: *Yet -*
Adrian: *Yet -*
Antonio: *He could not miss it.*
Adrian: *It must be of subtle, tender and delicate temperance.*

Shakespeare: *The Tempest*

Our determination to 'get on with it' was immediately thwarted the following morning when Nick had decided that we should make a joint ascent to the plateau (I emphasise that it was Nick who made the decision because I was somewhat lacking in enthusiasm, being still doubtful of my physical capabilities). Nelson took one look at the weather and said "No" and at that stage there were plenty of jobs crying out for attention on the hut-site in which we could all be usefully employed.

We were in the 'mild oceanic' Spring so we knew that the weather was bound to get progressively better and it was our discovery of the nature of the terrain which made the deepest impression first. After all,

Heigh-ho, the wind and the rain
For the rain it raineth, every day ..
It did.

'Heigh-ho, indeed,' I thought, stumping, nay, delicately placing my feet as I went along the shingle to recuperate our last pieces of cargo. In fact I was enjoying a freedom to move which was completely impossible round four-fifths of the periphery of the island because so much of it descends precipitously and inaccessibly to the sea.

The shingle beaches of the other fifth have no sand at all and are covered with wave-worn stones ranging in size from something like a fist to boulders within which one could accommodate a small garden shed. The initial choice of footwear lay between soft soles (trainers up to wellingtons) where the pain to the soles could prove exquisite, and boots (walking, climbing, mountaineering), where there was no danger to the soles but their added insensitivity made it more likely that one could sprain, twist or even break an ankle in one's progress from rock to rock. If one estimated one's maximum speed across the shingle at one and a half mph, this had to be reduced by a half when, as was frequently the case, it either was, or had been, raining.

If one paused in one's progress (as I did often), the variety of litter lying around was a source of continual amazement. Here we were on an uninhabited island, admittedly only thirty miles from a living community, but that the one which was supposed to be the most isolated community on earth, two thousand miles in any direction to anything comparable. What did we find on our shores? Apart from the 'gear of foreign dead men,' the great dark green glass floats encased in netting, the long orange and blue tangles of nylon rope lines, the indestructible luminous pink plastic spheres which were obviously replacing their glass ancestors, the rusty wreckage of old crayfish traps and plastic fish boxes, there was all kinds of strange debris. Ladies' sandals. used toothbrushes, bits of wiring, wood of various sizes ranging from the rectangular 'swing-seat' with a Japanese inscription which Nick found, to the capstan of some wreck which became a seat in the hut, to the enormous baulk of timber which Nelson and Andrew recuperated in late November with the intention of making two 'hoars' out of it, and by that time one could appreciate the need [See Plate 5]. All these were scattered sparsely along the shingle together with whale bones and teeth, rusting tins and the carcasses, more frequently the skeletons, of birds (usually prions) picked clean by the omnipresent Skua.

The brilliant emerald green Skua bog [See Plate 6] lay thirty yards in from the extremity of West Point and exercised a magnetic attraction for the Invertebrate Zoologist, the botanist and the ornithologist from a very early stage following the erection of the hut. Beneath the emerald carpet lay a rich brown mud with a distinctly nasty odour whose consistency varied from place to place, and from day to day. Frequent experiments by the Invertebrate Zoologist failed to produce penetration further than the crutch [*See Plate 6*]:for my own part, by dint of watching carefully where others put their feet, and by moving one step at a time, I avoided sinking further than ankle deep. A spice of interest could be added to one's cautious progress when it became necessary to take evasive action from the dive-bombing of angry Skuas but the ornithologist and his mate seemed to chart their way between the Scylla of the really soggy patches and the Charybdis of the Skuas with consummate ease, hence their speedy capture of a vagrant White-rumped Sandpiper in a mist net at the edge of the bog on the 1st November.

I am reliably informed that there are two 'roads' to the upper plateau of Inaccessible from the Blenden Hall promontory and during my excursions along the shingle in the direction of North Point and Tristan, I did indeed notice a possible ascent route which I suppose we might have attempted should an earthquake, landslip or eruption have obliterated our own, familiar, West Road.

It was on Sunday, 24 October, that Nelson decided that the weather was suitable for a joint ascent. Having come to the same conclusion about an hour and a half previously, I was not unprepared and we were able to set off by about 8.15, Nelson, wearing his moccasins, in the lead at a pace which looked like a gentle stroll. We threaded our way on a fairly mild slope through the tussock grass which was only waist-high in one or two places but was otherwise over our heads. It was not impenetrable but I was glad not to be the trail-blazer and concentrated on keeping my place about half-way down the line, where at least there was some indications of a route when the twistings and turnings of my immediate predecessor hid him from view. On one such occasion I stood for at least ten seconds boxing the compass before realising that he had disappeared into an unsuspected hole straight in front of me. Attempting to follow, I lost my footing and, to save my fall, clutched blindly at the surrounding tussock blades which promptly inflicted numerous minute lacerations on both my fingers and palms.

Skirting a canyon on our left and three apple trees in a hollow on our right, we reached a steep ascent of thick low heather/ scrub type vegetation where I was frequently reduced to progress on all fours when I was not clutching convulsively at some wind-shrivelled fern in the belief that I was about to fall backwards. (On future ascents, I never forgot to bring gloves, which became even more essential when the surveyor and his mate had put a fixed rope on this section.) We emerged to an open protuberance with rocks against which one could rest one's back - having realised that Nelson was doing just that, we collapsed gratefully. A five minute pause and we plunged back into the deep tussock, again ascending gently, but winding most unexpectedly and sometimes including the odd totally unforeseen descent. Crawling beneath the branches of an inconvenient Phylica, we emerged into an area where at least we could see a clear, if somewhat steep, undefined way upwards, and here again our generous guide granted a halt.

By this time the Expedition had become distinctly strung out and it would be dishonest were I not to admit that at that point I was concentrating on maintaining my position in the line and had totally forgotten the interests of the Expedition. I think that my record in the log reads somewhat as follows:

'Some of the younger generation drew further and further ahead, accompanied by their native guide, the senior scientists were delayed by interesting discoveries, and the older generation kept his head down and plugged away.'

I duly plugged upwards on a steep, bare slope, until our route verged to the right into a crevasse where we picked our way up to the left-hand side until we came level with some nesting Sooty Albatrosses on the opposite cliff, a most excellent excuse for another pause while photographs were taken [*See plate 7*].

The surveyor's mate, already knowing the route, was now considerably ahead, accompanied by the surveyor and Nelson. I was sticking with Andrew, Nick, Mike and a younger member solicitous about my decrepitude, while the Invertebrate Zoologist plus a couple of assistants grubbed away below.

We re-engaged ourselves upwards on a similar steep, tuft-covered slope, weaving our way from side to side and eventually reaching a point, quite suddenly, where we emerged on to an undulating level patch (about thirty metres below the edge of the plateau, hereinafter called 'Base') which extended some hundreds of metres in front us, eventually tapering off in the direction of Tristan.

A few minutes further repose and we scrabbled up the vertical, mud-covered final thirty metres, emerging on to a valley descending away from us covered with luxuriant grass which Nick immediately and triumphantly identified to me as 'Yorkshire Fog.' It had taken us over two hours to climb some four hundred metres, walking a distance of about a mile and, in my innocence, I was looking forward to striding across the central plateau, keeping a wary eye open for the peat bogs which had been advertised in one of our ornithological guides.

We moved up the slope to our right, picking our way between hidden burrows in the grass and the grey dolmen-like rocks, to be rewarded with a view of Nightingale Island some twelve miles away across the wine-dark sea which, from that height, looked calm, flat and inviting. The central plateau however, was anything but flat and we began to count the undulating valleys which stretched away from us in all directions, their similarity of appearance adding to our confusion. Beyond the cliffs to the north-east, the clouds and mist cleared intermittently, giving us occasional glimpses of Tristan towering out of the sea, while in the opposite direction Inaccessible rose to its highest point in the south-west corner [See plate 4].

We set off in that direction and quickly made the acquaintance of *Blechnum palinforme*, otherwise known as Tree Fern, an interesting plant which grew all over this area of the island. Shaped rather like a miniature palm tree, it generally reached some two feet in height and had a trunk about twice as thick as a man's leg. Such was its profusion, one could choose whether to thread one's way between the trunks or to use the umbrella shaped tops as stepping stones; in the latter case one was risking a sudden descent not of two feet, but of four, because the ground was thickly burrowed: if the burrow happened to be occupied, the indignant wails which arose provided an additional shock to the system. It turned out that some five or six valleys lay between us and the summit so on the return journey we decided to try walking along the cliff edge where there was no Tree fern and the irregularities of the terrain were less pronounced. If I had suffered the odd giddy moment when glancing backwards during the ascent, the sheer falls to my left which emerged from the increasing mist and low-lying cloud now took my breath away on several occasions before we reached the top of West Road: this was probably a good thing because the ensuing descent, though hard on the knees and ankles, seemed more like a gentle downhill stroll, except for those sections where tobogganing on the posterior seemed not only expedient but unavoidable. About two-thirds of the way home, I was slightly unnerved to hear a banshee-like scream from the upper regions, where the rear party was just beginning to come down, and was only reassured some ten minutes later when Mike identified the call of the Sooty Albatross ...

'Be not afeard - the isle is full of noises ...'

The isle, for its size, had a considerable range of vegetation in that the sheltered north eastern end was dominated by the Phylica tree, whereas the area we explored on that first day was dominated by the Tree fern and tussock. We did find two small peat bogs in the course of further exploration but the terrain overall varied very little from that which we encountered on 24 October and, once encountered, our attitude to it was modified from day to day not by its impenetrability, which we rapidly mastered or learned to live with, but by the ferocious changeability of the weather.

What was Matthew's quotation from Wordsworth on the 15 September?

There was a roaring in the wind all night
The rain came heavily and fell in floods ...

Whatever the evanescence of intimations of pre-cognitive experience, the rain certainly did on the evening and night following our first ascent when we were surprised to record half an inch of rain but this dribbled into insignificance when the same period between 5-6 November produced two and a half inches. It was over the previous night that Mike, Clive and Joe had camped on top of the island and had sat up from 2 am to 5 am taking twenty minute turns to hold the Force Ten tent masts in place but failing to prevent one of the masts from being bent irreparably out of shape; they had retreated at first light and spent most of the day recovering in the hut. By the night of the 6th, the gale had built up to new paroxysms of fury, a fury which we couldn't measure by conventional methods, though the inch of horizontal movement which I calculated in the kitchen end wall of the hut was a new record, a record with which we would have dispensed most willingly. The wind generator, which had been designed to make the maximum use of storm-force winds and gales, survived that night but was put out of action four nights later, whether by the action of the fresh gale or by collision with some helpless night bird we never discovered.

Personally I preferred the nights of rain to the nights of gales: during the former one would be kept awake by the tintinnabulation of raindrops leaking through the roof into strategically placed mess-tins but at least one had a fifty-fifty chance that one's bunk didn't lie beneath a leak, whereas during the latter one was constantly aware of the creaking and shifting of timbers, knowing that even if we survived the collapse of the hut around our heads, the other prong of Inaccessible's fork was exposure. On one occasion when my luck was out, (I had a fairly persistent dribble on to the middle of my upper spine for about three hours) I remember waking for about the sixth time at four o'clock in the morning, totally soaked and somewhat desirous of a personal leak: as my surrounding humidity was at least tepid, I preferred to lie there for another hour and a half before I ventured forth to relieve my then bursting bladder because I knew there was no way I could re-enter my sleeping bag once my body heat in it would have been dissipated. The same conditions prevailed the following night so I removed to the kitchen floor which proved surprisingly comfortable even if my sleeping-bag was still somewhat damp: there was lebensraum of which even Sylvie might have approved though I was by now accustomed to the narrowness of my very single bunk.

That the wind and the rain were so much a factor in our existence is borne out by figures I later obtained on Tristan about the month of November, when their fishermen would normally have expected to fish one day out of two. In November 1982, there were five 'fishing days,' but this was not the crucial factor in achieving the Expedition's frustration, much though we would have welcomed (supply-bearing) visitors from the outer world. We knew that it took the sea anything up to thirty-six hours to die down after adverse storms nor could anybody be unaware of the continuous pounding of the breakers fifty yards in front of us, even if I personally was also aware of the calm seas which invariably seemed to prevail at 6 am but which usually deteriorated within a couple of hours so that few other members saw them. Nevertheless some of us felt that our Island and naval friends might have made greater efforts to succour us, at least until 27 October, the day when the fishing boat 'Hilary' suddenly appeared round the north east point just after lunch-time. She went back round the point again only half-an-hour later, having made contact with our walkie-talkie (which at that time was somewhere on the top plateau) and having made all of us who were on the 'ground floor' fully conscious of the nature of the seas, which by that time we were beginning to take for granted: though only half a mile away, the three hundred and fifty ton vessel frequently disappeared from sight and her roll was such that the Invertebrate Zoologist averted his eyes.

Frustration finally lay in a combination of terrain and weather which was not violent but insidious. Though there were several days of rough weather and though the sea was impossible insofar as landing by dinghy was concerned for all but two days between the 16 October and 29 November (and it seemed fairly impossible on the latter day too), the most important factor in our lives was the fog/ mist/ low-lying cloud which hung over the top of the island on three days out of four up till Christmas. Once the hut was built, the plateau was where our scientists wanted to be: very often, it turned out to be where they couldn't go because, though conditions were satisfactory at sea-level, it was obvious that there would be no visibility up above. Even when the mountain cleared, it was often too late in the day for us to send people up who could achieve anything useful, apart from the 'sched' every forty-eight hours with Tristan, the responsibility for which gradually came to lie on my shoulders, accompanied by the faithful Gilfie.

Friday, 29 October was a fairly typical day because it comprised some kind of success with a feeling of not having achieved quite enough.

It had begun the previous day when Joe and Clive's effort to make an earth-oven had not succeeded - they were so crest-fallen and had put in so much work that when conditions seemed reasonable on the Friday morning, I volunteered to help them as a porter, while also doing the 'sched' later in the day. So we set off at about half-past nine, I, Clive, Joe, Andrew and Gilfie, all of us carrying quantities of equipment but Clive with three times as much as anybody else because it was the only way we could slow him down. The idea was that we would establish a camp for the surveyor and his mate, help them to chart a baseline and then the rest of us would descend once we had made contact with Tristan.

Slowly we picked our way in the warm Spring sunshine, pausing for fairly frequent rests and gradually shedding anoraks and jerseys. Only when we reached 'Base,' some thirty metres below the summit, about two hours later did we become aware of a freshening in the atmosphere, a freshening which suddenly changed into a chill and searching wind as we emerged on top. Hurriedly redonning all available garments, we scrambled over the slope to our left and descended into the valley stretching to the north. Here we chose a tent-site which seemed to afford the maximum shelter while lying close to a trickle of water (a most important consideration on top of the island). That particular stream flowed down to the sea just to the east of North Point at a cliff which later came to be designated 'Where the Pig fell off,' when Clive heard the story of how a party of islanders, sailing back to Tristan following a visit to Inaccessible after the Second World War, looked up to see a battle between two of the 'wild' pigs, which then lived on the island, taking place on top of that cliff: it was a battle which ended with the loser being unceremoniously pushed over the edge. No such source of meat now existed and we had to be content with two mugfuls of beef tea for lunch once the tent was erected. Joe, the surveyor's mate, clearly felt that as a tent resident, it was his job to do the cooking, so I sat on the edge of a small bank with the others, not exactly luxuriating because of the skeins of cloud which were now beginning to infiltrate our valley, but certainly enjoying the unusual feeling of not having a cooker to watch.

After lunch we applied ourselves to establishing the baseline. Clive had explained to me that he wanted to mark as long a straight line as possible across the highest possible stretch of ground and I had therefore suggested an army practice (I don't think I told him it was an army practice or he might have anathematised it immediately) by which we would station the two surveyors at either end of the chosen line while we three would endeavour to 'line up' on suitably chosen prominences in between. We worked out a series of simple signals to indicate 'Move right' or 'Move left;' then we all set off towards the tallest 'peak' which we could see centrally above us (later to be christened 'Cairn Peak'). From here we looked back along a ridge of minor peaks to 'Where the Pig fell off,' noticing gloomily the number of descents and ascents through the omnipresent Tree fern and the increasingly omnipresent wind-driven cloud. Leaving a marker pole on Cairn Peak we set off towards the next prominence on the ridge, from which we charted a route to the furthest prominence we could see. At this point we realised three things; first, that Joe would have to retrace his steps towards Cairn Peak in order to line me up with the furthest prominence, second, that Clive would have to progress a very long way to that point before we could start to line up our other members in between, and third, that we had very little chance of seeing either him or Joe at each end, never mind their signals, because of the ever-increasing cloud which continued to pile in from the south-west.

Nevertheless, Clive, accompanied by Gilfie, and Joe Solus set off in opposite directions while Andrew and I took shelter in the lee of our hill. Aeons of mist and solitude ensued, a phrase which I think is attributable to Major Sinclair Yeates, but at least he was riding a horse through an inhabited countryside when he employed it. After about half an hour we gave up trying to make conversation with each other and concentrated on huddling into our respective crevices; Joe was just visible on Cairn Peak but Clive and Gilfie had long since disappeared, as had Clive's destination, though I kept imagining I could see Gilfie's figure on one of the nearer intervening summits. My anxiety increased as the visibility decreased, an anxiety made the sharper because I was too well aware of the unreliability of compasses on Inaccessible: eventually I made violent beckoning gestures to Joe before he too disappeared from sight, gestures which he interpreted correctly because he rejoined us within twenty minutes and the three of us sat for another three-quarters of an hour before the other two, to my great relief, emerged from the mist. By now it was half-past three and we decided that enough was enough. Not without the odd detour, we retraced our steps to the tent and then climbed back up the slope above West Road in order to made the 'sched' with Tristan: luckily Gilfie had had the wit to note a position from which Tristan was visible on a previous occasion so we had no line of sight problems and we were able to make the ritual enquiries about our extra supplies and the availability of Royal Navy auxiliaries and receive the usual reassuringly cheerful vague promises from the other end. Then we three porters wished the two surveyors good luck and set off back to the hut, where I found that Nelson had been stocking up the larder with fish. The summary of that day in my diary reads:

'The continual cloud cover on top is going to be a bloody

nuisance. Otherwise I feel happier about the general situation.'

No doubt the happiness stemmed mainly from a sense of personal satisfaction at having managed the day's exercise without falling over and the 'general situation' had little to do with it.

The fact that we could only work on top of the island on about one day out of four meant that we got to know the Blenden Hall promontory very well indeed and that our life became progressively more 'comfortable' as we made improvements which we would not have had time to make if we had been able to get on with our proper work. There were, of course, some days when it was almost impossible to put one's head out of doors - the printable part of my diary for Monday 15 November runs as follows:

'It is 7.30 am as I write this - I have left breakfast to start late because it has been raining constantly since 2.20 am. Miraculously there were no drips over my bed but it has been a very disturbed night for some of the others. When the sky lightened a few minutes ago, Clive checked the rain-gauge - another two and a half inches, all of which has fallen since 2.20 am!'

'Another terrible day weatherwise - the wind was gusting violently at odd moments and there were frequent rainstorms. I spent most of the morning in the kitchen, not a penance on this occasion because everybody else was in the main room, where Joe was making a table out of the door to the scientist's den. Nick read John Buchan all morning apart from half an hour when he was hammering strips on to the roof, where the felt was threatening to fly away yet again. Lunch included twelve of yesterday's eggs fried, which made a pleasant change from the eternal soup and cheese. No 'sched' possible.

'Trousers damp all day from last night's bird-catching - long debate in the evening about the financial side of the trip - it became acrimonious and unpleasant, the first time this has happened, and so totally unnecessary. More bird-catching as the weather improved later on - several stormies, a lot of Softies, two prions but no shearwaters.'

More often I was recording days of further exploration of the Blenden Hall territory, of discoveries thereon, of successful larder-stocking activities and of activities within the hut such as the stamping and cacheting of several thousand envelopes, the product of the Inaccessible Post Office.

If Monday 15 November was a thoroughly gloomy day, Tuesday the 16th proved yet again the changeability of the climate; though the sea was very rough and there were occasional squalls of rain, everybody was able to achieve something positive. The surveyor and his mate departed up the mountain and soon after their departure the ornithologist at last accomplished the capture of an adult Rail. By the time he had brought it back to the hut to go through the measuring, weighing and photographic rituals, there were only his mate and Gilfie left to act as acolytes because the rest of us had departed in a northerly direction along the shingle, though in two groups with differing aims. The botanist, the Invertebrate Zoologist and their two mates intended to dig out the remains of a large fossilized tree which the botanist had discovered in a cave at Warren's Cliff a few days earlier. The size of the log indicated something far bigger than the island Phylica and the implications of the discovery were very exciting from a scientific viewpoint: my own excitement was caused by the prospect of an egg-hunting foray (see Chapter 9) with Nelson and Andrew. The shearwater colony was the same one I had visited with Andrew on Remembrance Sunday but I was inveigled by the others into visiting the fossilised tree some quarter of a mile further along the shingle before having to retrace my steps to rejoin our guides. They would already be deeply ensconced in the burrows by the time I got back.

"How will I find you?" I enquired nervously.

"Holler," they answered, and disappeared, on all fours.

My salaams to the fossilised wood were fairly perfunctory but by the time I got back to the colony. Nelson and Andrew had completely disappeared. By dint of tracking the sections of disturbed soil and by fairly desperate 'hollering' (the noise of the surf was deafening), I finally made contact and participated in a successful hunt which produced seventy-seven eggs and, right at the end, a dozen shearwaters for the pot.

The shearwater curry that night went well with macaroni and baked beans and the serving thereof was particularly easy because it all came from one big plastic bucket; furthermore, there was even enough for 'seconds.' After dark we (I and the ornithologist) caught two White-faced Storm Petrels and two Great Shearwaters and my diary for that day concludes:

'A good day and a fine night, auguring well for the 'sched' tomorrow, but you never know.'

In fact, the following day was also fine as was most of Thursday the 18th. On the Wednesday, the surveyors went up the mountain again and the guides and I indulged our cynegetic instincts in an enormous tramp southward along the shingle to almost the farthest point one could reach, before plundering the shearwater colony at that end. This exploit produced a further seventy eggs for the larder but we did not get back until half-past one and I was glad that I had warned Nick about lunch for the remainder, most of whom had gone off to explore the only available rock-pool, just a few hundred yards along the shingle in a northern direction.

The surveyor's mate did the 'sched' and returned with the information that if the weather continued fair, the barge from Tristan might be coming 'tomorrow.' In this case, I and the Invertebrate Zoologist could even be required to return with it in view of the uncertainty of the South Atlantic Spring. We learnt that President Breznev had died and that England were losing a Test Match in Australia.

That evening was very convivial until a mild argument about the value of our stamp covers was effectively and efficiently settled by Nick. Nobody was sure if that might not be the last night, for some of us ...

The fine calm of the next day, the 18 November, induced the surveyor, his mate and the ever-willing Ian to set off up the mountain with the intention of spending at least two nights on top. The ornithologist and his mate disappeared in the direction of the Skua Bog, though their goal was the Phylica behind the bog where Wilkin's Buntings had been located. Our guides, perhaps deceived by the continuing fine weather, went off on another egg hunt, which this time was for the benefit of their respective wives in the event of the barge arriving, but they conscientiously fished for the Expedition larder in the afternoon. Shearwater eggs scrambled proved a great success for lunch and were relatively easy with a clientèle of only seven.

I spent most of the afternoon tidying the beach but also watched the fishing and took photos of a fur seal which was clearly enjoying the sunshine and felt as lazy as I did. Later in the evening the weather broke and we recorded another inch of rain overnight. That was the end of the only three days of more or less continuous fine weather that we experienced in six weeks.

Fog and mist were our lot the following morning but we were less inclined to be anxious about the three on the mountain because of previous experiences. Water dripped through the roof for most of the day but we managed some local bird-watches and Andrew produced thirty shearwaters which were fumigated to collect insect parasites and measured before I was allowed to start culinary operations. Considerable philatelic and epistolary activity continued; the three from the mountain walked in soaked at about 5pm.

For the next week the weather followed the same daily pattern: a calm sea when I got up at 6 am but fog, mist and cloud on the mountain. The sea would get rougher by about eight but the weather on Blenden Hall would gradually improve and we had several lovely afternoons which provoked visits to the plateau, even though the time available for scientific work was much shorter. Increasing fitness and knowledge of the route made the ascent much quicker: what started as a two-hour ascent was reduced to thirty-four minutes by one of the young men and even I managed it in forty-nine in late November. Thus afternoon visits became viable and were accomplished several times though the surveyor and his mate were the most likely to be made redundant through poor visibility.

Sooty Albatross on nest.

Expedition about to sail from Capetown

A Corner of the Kitchen.

"The shearwaters are supper and you're cooking them"

CHAPTER 6

CHARACTER IS DESTINY

Ainsi fallait-il me résigner, puisque rien ne peut durer qu'en devenant général et si l'esprit ment à soi-meme, à l'idée que même les être qui furent les plus chers à l'écrivain n'ont fait en fin de compte que poser pour lui comme chez les peintres.

Proust: Le Temps Retrouvé

And I had to resign myself, since nothing can last except by becoming general (unless the mind lies to itself), by accepting the idea that even those beings who were dearest to the writer have ultimately only posed to him as for painters.

There is a slide [*See plate 8*] which I normally use to introduce the members of the Expedition whenever I have to give a talk on the subject. It shows the ten of us standing in front of the bows of the *Agulhas* on the afternoon of the 6 October about an hour before sailing and I usually read from right to left, giving our ages, normal occupations and Expedition occupations. Even though I am standing second from the left, I leave my own details to the last in order that the words 'forty-six' point the difference between me and the next oldest, Nick (thirty) and between Nick and the youngest member, Gilfie (sixteen). If this raises a laugh, it is very welcome at an early stage in the lecture, but it illustrates the very serious pleasure with which Elizabeth Swales greeted the news that I was joining the Expedition.

"You will," she said, "be someone for Mike to talk to ..."

If I suffered from loneliness when Mike was forced to drop out, this was no fault of the other members and might well have been my own, though I would prefer to attribute it to the 'age-gap.'

*   *   *

Even though Mike Fraser, our ornithologist at four days notice, is standing slightly apart on the right of the slide, he seemed to have no difficulty in bridging the gap between himself and the other nine 'Denstonians.' His ability to learn quickly and to get on with other people was proved within the twenty-four hours of our sailing from Cape Town, by which time his contribution to the untidiness of the cabin which he shared with Richard, Ian and Gilfie, had at least equalled theirs; moreover he had become distinctly persona grata with the four ornithologists from the University of Cape Town, en route to Gough Island. (Mike, in April 1984, was researching at the Percy Fitzpatrick Institute of African Ornithology as a direct result of the Denstone Expedition - Honi soit qui mal y pense.)

A son of the Manse, he had started by reading English Literature at his Scottish University, but after a year, had been allowed to change to Zoology/ Biology because of his passionate interest in birds. Thoroughly professional in his attitude, he was prepared to go to any lengths in the pursuit of his researches but had the maturity to know what was unreasonable. In his view, it was totally unreasonable that the Expedition should be 'dry' and he was good enough to make his position on this matter crystal clear. ("If I've been watching birds for five hours in a peat bog, I'm having a whisky when I come in!")

As Nick and I had already discussed this particular subject at some length, and had come to Mike's conclusion, we were only too happy to concur. Mike's authority grew as the younger members learnt to know him and to respect his ability and judgement: even though he and Richard Preece complained on one occasion that they were not getting enough assistance, Mike soon had nearly everybody trained in the arts of 'watching,' ringing, handling and observing; on at least two occasions it was his tart intervention which saved me the necessity of giving tongue, the said interventions being that much more effective in that coming from Mike, they were totally unexpected. Devoted though he was to his subject and despite an age-gap of twenty years, he several times made a point of asking me to accompany him on ornithological projects and it was no coincidence that these invitations seemed to occur whenever I was beginning to feel the strain of responsibility or of frustration. His control of his own frustration when one of the younger members in the top bunk vomited all over him as he took cover below was admirable.

"Why didn't you get out of the way?" Nick asked him.

Mike considered for a moment and then replied:

"When the enemy's that close, you keep your head down and wait for him to exhaust his ammunition!"

His contributions to the Log were always amusing, particularly after the night he and the cartographers spent holding up the tent on top of the island. They had passed some of the time inventing gastronomic delights, Mike's suggestions being of the 'Fillet Steak on Raquel Welch's navel' order, but his total contribution on that day spread over four foolscap pages. Typical passage:

'0111 and 10 seconds, 'Classical Choice:' A selection of your serious favourites: *Handel's Water Music* played, for the first time as it was intended - under water by the Inaccessible Trio. *The Swan* by Saint-Saens (from *Carnival of the Animals*). The composer's wistful evocation of the pristine swan gliding gracefully across the placid waters of a calm lake. It feeds delicately, swallows some lead shot, becomes water-logged and drowns. *Land of mountain and flood*, Mendelssohn's stirring description of Inaccessible Island. The *Trout Quintet* by Schubert. This proud and fighting fish is pictured masterfully by the composer, swimming strongly through the rapids. Suddenly it is caught in violent spate and swept into a tent occupied by three ravenous explorers, who eat it. *Variations on British Sea Shanties* by Benjamin Britten. Includes such popular airs as *What shall we do with a drunken Explorer?* and *Bobby Shaftoe's gone to sea*, arrives at Inaccessible and is banished by the natives for wearing silver buckles on his knee and thereby being a raging poofter.' *Theme from Onedin Line* by Katchachurian. The fine clipper sails the Seven Seas through storm and gale. One day, many miles from home and therefore not having had it in months, the crew come across Flora MacDonald who has missed Skye and ended up in the South Atlantic. Being otherwise engaged, the crew failed to notice Inaccessible, run aground, and the ship is lost with all hands.

'0300, 'Shakespeare for a wet day' presented by the All-Inaccessible Underwater Formation Dancing Team, while clutching a tentpole in a force ten gale in three feet of water. *The Merchant of Venice* in which Shylock demands his pound of flesh, rare to medium, with mushrooms, broccoli, french fries and a bottle of Nuit Saint Georges 1976.'

When it became clear that Richard and I would be departing in the near or far future with, among many other things, letters to everybody's nearest and dearest, it emerged that Mike had twenty-six of these (compared with about five per other member). Certainly the top letter was addressed to his parents at the Manse: discretion forbade that I should examine the twenty-five below.

When I had finished the 'Bird' chapter in this book (chapter 8), I sent it to Mike for comments. My six thousand word chapter came back some fortnight later with sixty-one carefully typed annotations, many of them informative, many making minor corrections or emendations and at least three complimentary. Some of his comments have survived in the final text, but my wife's remark after she had taken an entirely private and unauthorised peek at the chunks of typescript lying about on my desk was, as usual, relentlessly Gallic:

'If you ever publish that chapter, you must publish not only his comments but your comments on his comments!'

Next to Mike in the photo stands Joe Dakin, who was christened Jonathan but who took strong exception to being inscribed 'Jo' in the Log because, he insisted, this was a girl's name. Pointing out to him that Joe was an abbreviation for Joseph made as little impression as any of my other literary/ syntactical or artistic observations made on any other members of the Expedition, so that it was obvious that in such a personal matter, the claims of scientific terminology could be waived.

Joe's forte was his ability to use his hands and his weakness, perhaps, his inability to stop talking when there was nothing to occupy his hands. He was never happier than when he was rummaging about in the hold of the *Agulhas* counting bits of wood or when we were erecting the hut in our first week on the island, except, unfortunately, when his pleasure in vocal rows impinged on the susceptibilities of some members more sensitive than Joe's chief, Clive, who was quite capable of giving as good as he got.

His immense practical ability meant that Joe made an immediate rapport not only with the seamen on the *Agulhas* but also with our Tristan guides: he had such a continuous need of jobs if he were not on the plateau surveying, that sometimes one was forced to invent them. I still reproach myself for the fact that the Inaccessible shower, the product of Joe's inventive genius, did not come into use until the 25 November: there had been so many days when I might have directed willing hands in that direction and it was a great improvement in the washing facilities. His ability to make contact with people extended to the walkie-talkie, which had been placed in his charge when it was delivered two hours before our departure on 2 October but, though he could make the thing work, this was less of a success because he could not realise that changing the times of 'scheds' might not be convenient on Tristan (this was one of the reasons for the nine days silence which was eventually broken by Hilary's siren on 27 October). Even when in contact, Joe was inclined to suppose that the whole resources of Tristan da Cunha and Tristan Investments Ltd. were entirely at the Expedition's service, which led to several unnecessary misunderstandings: it was only gradually, with the loyal aid of Gilfie, that I managed to make the 'sched' chore my own and clarify the real nature of our problems to the ever-faithful Richard Grundy on Tristan.

The one place where Joe seemed somewhat impractical was the kitchen: he spent considerable time and effort making me a desk there when it became clear that the Invertebrate Zoologist had established a monopoly over the desk in the scientist's room, he built shelves for me to store cooking essentials, and it was he who spent a whole afternoon cleaning the stove and trimming its wicks but, as a farmer's son, he believed that cooking was not a man's job and he had a strong aversion for it. One of the few occasions when I lost my cool and my eirenic propensities deserted me was when he refused to take his place on the 'Cook's assistant' rota because he felt he was doing more important work on the survey. I remember observing to him rather sourly that he was very good at doing things he liked doing and bloody awful at doing things he didn't like, so it was twelve days before he volunteered to make the bread, an offer which I gratefully, and I hope gracefully, accepted.

One of Joe's more tiresome habits was to try to needle the young man who is standing next to him in the photograph, David Briggs. Another farmer's son, David was mild in temperament, very good-looking and immensely strong; so strong that he could easily have picked Joe up and thrown him in the sea: it is a sad comment on my own generation that his would undoubtedly have been Joe's fate twenty years earlier but David was quite impervious to the teasing, just as he seemed impervious to the weather when he was doing bird-watches. Apart from his practical ability in the construction of the hut, this was David's great contribution to the success of the Expedition: under Mike's tutelage he would spend hour after hour recording the doings of Tristan Thrushes and Tristan Buntings and there were many times when he came in with rain sluicing off his anorak and lines of weariness on his face. The only time I remember David becoming even mildly angry was on 17 November when there was an argument about the price of stamp covers to members of the Expedition; it is perhaps an interesting reflection that the only general rows which occurred were both about money. It was no accident that David was chosen to accompany me to Tristan for our three-hour visit on 16 October, nor was I at all surprised to learn that he accumulated a large number of lady admirers during the five weeks that the Expedition was stranded on Tristan after Christmas.

In front of David stands the other David who was known as Gilfie. Bespectacled, small in stature and the youngest member (just sixteen), Gilfie had worked all through the summer holidays in a store in Texas in order to earn the money to pay his share of the Expedition. Another good-humoured, patient young man, it was difficult to shake his equanimity and he accepted the post as my assistant without demur, the pairing of the oldest and the youngest member being quite fortuitous. I have forgotten how many times Gilfie and I climbed West Road together to do the 'sched,' just as I have forgotten how many times he was the last to arrive for breakfast porridge: even though we were inclined to go to sleep comparatively early (this was a policy decision in order to make maximum use of daylight hours) there were times when I wondered if he was getting enough sleep. Nick and I became concerned about a mysterious stomach complaint from which he started to suffer, round about 22 November, which was just after a telex from Mike Swales had informed us that he was coming out in January and that the *HMS Endurance* was due to pick up the whole Expedition in mid-February en route to the Falklands: on 21 November, I wrote in my diary:

'Some of the young men are beginning to realise just how long they are going to be on the island now that Mike is coming in January and there seems little chance of their being home before March. It is making them a little bit thoughtful. If something doesn't come from Tristan this week, I shall be thoughtful too.'

On 26 November, I warned Peter Warren on *Tristania II* that we might need to evacuate Gilfie but the state of the sea on that day made any such idea totally impractical. In fact we took him with us on 29 November and he made a speedy recovery on Tristan, where he settled in with Richard Grundy, making himself generally useful in the ensuing weeks leading up to Christmas. He distinguished himself on 4 December at the dance to celebrate the farmer's departure when he accepted an invitation to the Pillow Dance (described later), much to the delight of everybody present. He also accepted the challenge of going back to 'school' in May 1983, which can't have been at all easy after having been treated as an adult for the previous six months.

The most intellectually and academically distinguished of the young men was Richard 'Dick' Holt, who stands next in the straggly multi-coloured line. Apart from his ability in scientific subjects, Dick had considerable musical gifts and a working knowledge of many other subjects (even including French!) Despite his seasickness, which kept him in his bunk for some time during the outward voyage, obviously he was the junior member whom I learnt to know best at the beginning of the Expedition as he was sharing a cabin with Nick and myself. Apart from his job as assistant Postmaster and 'Guardian of the Stamp,' which he and Chief Postmaster Nick had plenty of time to discuss and plan, it was Dick who became Richard Preece's assistant in the Department of Invertebrate Zoology. He helped Richard to collect geological specimens and his knowledge of physics provided a useful theoretical foil to Ian's practical ability in making the wind generator work.

Just as Dick's academic standards were high, so were his standards of morality and hygiene but if there was a touch of self-righteousness in some of his comments in the Log, the comments frequently proved most timely (as did his efforts to sweep the floor of the hut). The other members accepted the sincerity of his faith, nor did anybody ever question his 'privileged' position in our cabin, if indeed it were ever considered 'privileged.' It was Dick who recorded his enjoyment of the hymn-singing during the Sunday service on *Agulhas* and Dick who occasionally, diffidently, read us the Collect for the day whenever anybody remembered that it was Sunday morning (the son of the Manse showed little enthusiasm for that particular chore).

I remember sharing his relief when, on 10 October, he and I succeeded in making the ship's automatic laundry deal with our accumulated dirty washing: it was not until a month later on a bread-making occasion that I realised that my own fears about hygiene in the kitchen were magnified in Dick's mind by about two hundred percent.

Having counted the number of washing-up cloths and the number of pan-scourers (three) very soon after landing, I had decided unilaterally that I would be responsible for the washing-up of all kitchen and cooking utensils after every meal, though each member would be responsible for his own mess-tins, mug, knife, fork and spoon. I made the mistake of announcing that this was the British Army method, as practised in my youth, which caused great offence to Clive, but it seemed to work and at least

I was satisfied with, and had confidence in, the saucepans I was using. If members later suffered from food-poisoning because of the state of their own mess-tins, that was their own look-out ... and how one or two of them escaped stomach upsets, I shall never know. Jealously I conserved my pan-scourers for the heavy work, encouraging bids for the right to 'scrape the saucepan' at every meal, cheerfully volunteering my own mess-tin for the bread-making because at least I knew it was clean ...

All had gone well until the day when whoever's turn it was to make the bread grabbed the absent Dick's clean mess-tin as one of those available in which to perform the operation. Normally, either I or the bread-maker had time to clean out the bits of burnt crust which adhered to the sides and bottom of the tin once the loaf had been turned out but on this occasion I was busily engaged in cooking and the bread-maker had been urgently summoned elsewhere when Dick returned and discovered his unclean mess-tin. Very politely, he asked me for one of my precious pan-scourers and when, reluctantly, I proffered the oldest and tiredest of my collection, he proceeded to spend some eighteen minutes meticulously restoring his tin to its pristine condition ...

He was, however, the only one of us to spend long periods of time within the first penguin rookery, which was possibly the most insalubrious of all terrains on the island and where he was hoping to do a study of the underside wing patterns of the Rockhopper. After considerable efforts, this study unfortunately had to be abandoned because he had neglected to mark the penguins which he had already examined, a most unscientific lapsus on Dick's part.

His bunk lay under Clive's, at the back of the hut, and I cherish the memory of one evening when we were nearly all in bed and were having a conversation on a non-scientific topic about which I knew something. Pedantically, I corrected somebody who made an error of fact or terminology, to receive the impatient retort:

"John, you're a typical schoolmaster!"

Cavernously from the depths of Dick's bunk there came the

solemn, portentous words:
"He's not."

It was one of the few unsolicited compliments I received but maybe it wasn't meant as a compliment.

The two Richards worked well together and are standing next to each other in the slide. The senior Richard, who appears rather frequently in this book as the Invertebrate Zoologist as well as under his own name, was very vague about most things in life, even meal-times. He seemed to have wandered into the Expedition almost accidentally but his immense good nature was of enormous benefit to the atmosphere within the group. It took him hours to get ready before he could set off anywhere but he didn't mind being teased by the young and his perception of their strengths and weaknesses often helped to open new perspectives to me. Even though he often arrived late for meals, he ate his full share and it was a source of some amazement to us all that he could eat three large meals per day even when prostrated with seasickness.

Where insects and snails were concerned, Richard had tunnel vision and apart from spending long hours investigating their presence on the island, he would expound the needs of Invertebrate Zoology (and Geology) whenever he felt the occasion warranted exposition. Not the quickest of movers, whenever he set off in a group he would inevitably gravitate to the rear as he stopped to grub about in the soil and we soon became accustomed to ascertaining his location by his posterior, which fortunately was large enough to be picked out from a considerable distance. Once the scientists' room had been established at the far end of the hut, its writing desk conveniently situated beneath the solitary window, it quickly became apparent to the other three senior scientists that they were fighting a losing battle if they thought that they were allowed to share more than a quarter of the available space among the three of them. Nick realised this so quickly that he kept his flower-presses under his bunk in the main room, doing all his work on them and all his philatelic work on my bunk: Mike seemed to manage most of his bird-measuring in one corner, and Clive moved most of his heavy surveying equipment to a cache on the upper plateau, where he left it.

I had observed this process with some amusement until the 26 October, when I discovered that one of my two precious plastic buckets (from which dinner was frequently served) had disappeared from the kitchen. Upon investigation, I found it in the scientist's room, full of seaweed. In that particular case my outraged protest was accepted and the theft was not repeated but Dr. Preece continued totally ruthless in the appropriation of any equipment or material which he judged suitable for his researches and he was similarly determined to maintain his position on any subject when he knew he was in the right. When noises began to emanate from Expedition headquarters in England during the second half of November to the effect that only Woolley should be returning on the *Tristania II*, Richard quietly reminded me and Nick of the assurance that we three had received on 1 October that 'whatever happened' we should be home by 3 January, and he maintained his position with dignity, without complaint or recrimination.

Nick Hall, next in the photo line, had been equally embarrassed by the 3 January assurance and as he was the only leader to accomplish the whole duration of the Expedition, it is fitting to record this fact immediately as a tribute to his courage, pertinacity and perseverance. Even though he was the member that I knew best and from whom I had few secrets, I think that he would find it easier to write about me than I do to write about him. He had a doctor's gift for understanding people but his scorn of outward appearances (which I shared) was accompanied normally by a diffident approach to new acquaintances who were therefore inclined to underestimate the steely determination beneath the mild exterior. At the beginning he knew far more about the members of the Expedition than I did and infinitely more about its scientific objectives, but he was not used to giving orders and expecting to be obeyed. Nor was he used to interviewing people and having to sum up their attitudes and prejudices quickly enough to be able to influence them sympathetically towards one's own objectives, and, though I cannot remember how early he asked me to become 'Co-' rather than 'Deputy' Leader, I am sure that the only reason he did so was because he thought I had some ability in coercing people, particularly those of my own generation.

During the first telephone call when we became acquainted, we had come to an immediate understanding on the necessity for medicinal alcohol and on 1 October, one of our first joint decisions was to lift the embargo on alcohol, depending on availability and baggage allowance. If this seemed a hair-raising change from the original plan, it was nothing compared with the ideas which Nick could calmly produce when faced with a problem.

2300 hours. 2 October. In flight between Heathrow and Abidjan.

JW: "What are we going to do if they charge us hundreds of pounds for excess baggage on the Johannesburg - Cape Town flight?"

Nick : "We'll send the rest of the lads on by air and you and I will hire a van in Johannesburg, using our Barclaycards as security, and then drive to Cape Town."

JW (weakly): "Oh!"

2200 hours. 3 October. Expedition meeting in Helmsley Hotel, Cape Town. Nick addressing all members on inherent dangers once landed on Inaccessible Island.

Nick : "If anybody suffers a serious injury, even something like a broken leg, you probably won't survive."

JW (mentally): "Oh!"

Quiet and often indecisive, Nick became quite definite once the chips were down. On 17 November, when he had laid out all the stamp-covers for members to look at and make their orders (he was giving us first choice) the usual vocal minority protested that members should not pay the full price. Nick let them talk for about half an hour, took the orders from those members who had already made up their minds and then calmly swept all the covers away and went to bed. Within the next forty-eight hours every member had placed his order.

He liked to have time to prepare for future events and his preparation of his botanical specimens and of the stamp-covers was as meticulous as Dick's but he seemed to take more delight from success: on 4 November his pleasure at having found the Inaccessible 'Pepper Tree' (*Pepperonia Tristanensis*) was as infectious as the joy he got from making perfect stamp-covers. His explanation of the art of bread-making together with the properties of live and dried yeast to the young men was so clear that, for a short time, even I understood it, even though I never understood why it took Nick almost as long as Richard Preece to get ready to go up the mountain. If my own authority stemmed spuriously from my age and habituation to being obeyed, in Nick's case it came from his ability to make the correct practical suggestion at the right moment. After four weeks on the island when he realised that the commissariat was under control and that the cook needed a change of scene, he made a point of including me in a botanical expedition to the apple trees, where we fossicked happily for a couple of hours, spring blossoms over our heads and last year's apples covering the ground. A Noddy discovered us and we didn't discover anything but the immediate benefit to my morale was figured in that evening's dinner when we indulged in the unheard of luxury of an 'entrée' (fish cakes) and the long-term effect to make me aware of my own need to get out of the kitchen and do something different, particularly in the afternoons.

Nick and I are standing fairly forward in the picture and between us in the background stands Clive, his round, indecisive features belying his position as the self-appointed 'conscience' of the Expedition. He had been landed with the complete responsibility for making the map at very short notice and it soon became obvious that he had not been expecting the Expedition to leave at all "Who had?" [*Helpful comment from Co-leader*], such was his lack of personal preparation and his apparent ignorance of the carefully typed sheets of instructions. Nevertheless he had brought enough cartographic books to learn as he went along: moreover he had the sense to check the theodolite in Cape Town, a most fortunate foresight in view of its faulty condition. Though Clive was the first and the quickest to make criticisms of the lack of equipment:

2130 hours. 3 October. Meeting in Helmsley Hotel. Cape Town:
Clive: "You can't call a black plastic dustbin liner a survival bag!"
Nick: "You can call it what you bloody well like but its what you're

going to have to survive in". And though his idea of taking democratic decisions was of the usual undergraduate variety, his devotion to the ideals of the Expedition was whole-hearted and unswerving. Apart from his strength and endurance, he had some mountaineering experience and he carried great quantities of equipment up to the top of the island, making, with Joe, far more ascents than any other member of the Expedition. He was as much a perfectionist as the other senior scientists and it was a source of some dismay to his assistant when a whole series of survey readings turned out to be faulty; the consequence was a patient, laborious and exhausting revisiting of all the sites concerned. When it was necessary to make accurate measurements in the area of the Skua Bog, there was no question of skirting round the edge: I have vivid visual and olfactory memories of Clive and Joe returning muddied to the navel after a mapping exercise on 13 November.

His great virtue was his basic good nature and his ability to remain cheerful, even when the main leak through the roof of the hut led directly down the wall through his bunk for a period of some five days. Apart from myself, he was usually the first to get up in the morning and when I heard him making his way to the rain-gauge, singing his five-note theme song to himself, I would put out his mess tin with his ration of dry porridge oats: for some reason he didn't like cooked porridge but as I didn't like porridge at all I could hardly question his taste. Like Joe, he was very practical and took as much pleasure in the construction of a dry stone loo on the beach as he did in writing out the 'Rules for the Karzie.' His contributions to the Log did not need his signature: their ingenuousness and the forcefulness of the language were unmistakable. It was Clive who, on first sighting Inaccessible, described it as 'beautiful' which was not an epithet which came to anybody else's mind on that particular day. On one evening when I was justifying the teaching of Shakespeare to fifteen-year olds, a pedantic necessity of which he clearly disapproved, he listened to my reasons and promptly borrowed my complete Shakespeare in order to reread *Richard II*, which again was not a reaction I would have expected from any other Expedition member. In one sense he was perhaps the most conservative of the group because he found it most difficult to adapt to a different style of leadership and he was the most concerned about the possibility of an early departure during the first three weeks on the island: when, on the other hand, it began to appear in mid-November that the return journey would involve a visit to the Falkland Islands with the Royal Navy he became gravely concerned as this, in his view, would have involved him in serious loss of face among his undergraduate friends in Leeds!

On the extreme left of the slide stands the last of the young assistants, Ian Best, the practical physicist. Equipped with an expensive camera, his lack of concern when his expensive spectacles dropped off his nose into the ocean on the third day of the voyage of the *Agulhas* had given Nick uneasy qualms about the advisability of issuing him with too many rolls of Expedition film, but in the end his photographic record was more complete than anybody else's and probably constitutes his most important single material contribution to the Expedition. Ian was amiably willing to help anybody with anything but was so self-effacing that I only began to appreciate his true worth rather late in the day when he offered to keep an eye on the commissariat after my departure. Maybe my early doubts stemmed from the saga of his order for 'alcohol from bond' of which my notebook still preserves the record.

Once Captain Leith had given us the nod to make our order from the ship's bond supplies (as recounted in Chapter 4). I took individual orders from each member before presenting the total requirement to the steward. Ian's initial order was half a case of vodka and half a case of gin, but then it occurred to him that these drinks required excessive amounts of tonic water or bitter lemon. so this order is scratched out and further down the page one reads: 'Ian Best:
3 bottles rum, 2 bottles whisky, 1 bottle gin,4 cases Castle Lager.'
What happened to make him change his mind again I don't know but there is another line crossing out the whole order and beside

it is written tersely : '½ case rum.'

One evening after we had been on the island for about three weeks, Ian appeared morosely beside me in the kitchen with an open bottle of rum in his hand.

"Have a drink, John," he said, and when I had willingly taken the ritual swallow from the neck of the bottle, he departed equally morosely, observing over his shoulder:

"I don't like rum ..."

At different times Ian assisted in the collection of geological specimens, was always concerned with the working of the wind generator, helped the cartographers as a willing porter, spent hours trying to catch and photograph the Inaccessible Rail as well as doing many bunting watches, constructing the patent Inaccessible oven out of an empty paraffin tin and achieved the record time to the top of the island of thirty-four minutes on 27 November (he gave me ten minutes start as pacemaker and overtook me somewhere near the Sooty Albatrosses - in my efforts NOT to be overtaken, I achieved my own personal best: forty-nine minutes.)

His versatility was demonstrated when, after eight days of cheese and biscuits for lunch, he and Clive were responsible for making the first 'chapattis;' some seven months later it was Ian and Gilfie who came to stay with me in Yorkshire in order to help with the cataloguing of about seven thousand slides.

*   *   *

Is there an unseen presence hovering somewhere in that slide: an apparently omniscient, optimistic, teetotal presence blithely administering his Benedicite ('No problem') or cheerfully advocating the advantages of 'Plan B'? I never asked Mike Swales how far down the alphabet I ranked as an alternative 'Plan' and he would probably be too tactful to tell me but there is no doubt that his absence left a gaping hole in our leadership which Nick and I only cobbled over very gradually. Somewhere in my diary there is a note in favour of the evening 'tot' which reads:

"I don't think I would have survived if this Expedition had been really 'dry' but of course if Mike had been there, I wouldn't have the responsibility."

So much of the planning and logistics was in Mike's head that I still laugh rather bitterly when I look at the two and a half pages of notes scribbled into an exercise book on 1 October though the gap was not just an administrative one. We were made forcibly aware of Mike's standing as an ornithologist on the first day of the voyage of the *Agulhas*: the bird men from the University of Cape Town were greatly disappointed not to find the author of the standard 'Seabirds of Gough Island' among our number. Even if Mike Fraser plugged the ornithological gap with distinction, Mike Swales remained omnipresent in our minds and in our day-to-day conversation: it is so much easier to swear at an absentee leader when things go wrong!

I had a long list of faults, errors, missing pieces of equipment and essential extra requirements when I landed at Heathrow on 18 December and I remember one moment when, after about twelve hours talking, Mike finally interrupted me.

"You keep telling me about the transport difficulties and communication difficulties," he said. "I can't understand why you keep referring to the beginning of the Expedition as 'chaos.' Didn't any of you have any faith?"

At that moment it did not occur to me to tell him that the two people in whom Nick and I had faith throughout our joint leadership were our two Tristan guides, Nelson Green and Andrew Glass, who joined us on the day we landed on Inaccessible and who therefore do not figure in the Cape Town slide. From the point of view of any lecture I might give, this is probably a good thing because my 'forty-six' paled into insignificance besides Andrew's 'fifty-six' and Nelson's 'sixty-seven;' from the point of view of the success of the Expedition, I think that without their presence we might have had to evacuate at least half the members back to Cape Town prior to Christmas.

Nelson and Andrew knew instinctively what the weather was doing even if they didn't understand why we were enduring the worst South Atlantic spring for some twenty years. Faced with the vagaries of nature, they were not perturbed and preserved a monumental calm, a calm whose taciturnity I would have been glad to break in order to find out what they were really thinking. They never told us things which we didn't ask about. When I was back on Tristan, I did a tour of Marie-José's gardens where her gardener pointed out a Cape Gooseberry bush (*Physalis peruviana*) and told me roughly where a similar plant existed on Inaccessible. The following day I passed on this information in the 'sched,' only to be presented two days later with a "We can't find it, it's not there." When we were having lunch with Nelson we told him about the missing gooseberry bush, only to be informed that Nelson KNEW it wasn't there because he and Andrew had been to look for it. When we asked why they hadn't told us about it, their answer was irrefutable - why talk about it if it isn't there? [*The Cape Gooseberry was rediscovered on Inaccessible in February 1983*].

Though they had some reservations about lentils, they ate everything I provided, assuring me that it was 'fine,' 'OK,' 'good,' and having to be persuaded to accept their fair share of 'seconds' on the rare occasions when these were available. It was only after Christmas that Nelson's reputation as a cook came to light as did the fact that he was a superb helmsman; none of us knew that Andrew was Tristan's leading shepherd until we saw him directing operations on sheep-shearing day.

Being less ecologically minded than my scientific brethren, I was in sympathy with our guide's predatory instincts and certainly shared their determination to survive. We enjoyed hunting and fishing together and even though their skills far surpassed mine, we shared the same thrill in a successful capture, whether it was for 'ringing' purposes or for the pot. Their ability to make use of almost all kinds of flotsam and jetsam washed up on the shingle was only defeated by the fluorescent plastic floats which have now replaced the beautiful dark green glass floats encased in netting of which we found a considerable number. I treasure the memory of Nick's face when, on 24 October, having climbed to the highest point of Inaccessible, Nelson passed round two cans of beer to celebrate the ascent and, when they were finally returned to him empty, tossed them casually into the surrounding Tree fern.

We only realised how deeply they felt about the Expedition when, having unexpectedly announced their intention of returning to Tristan with Richard, Gilfie and me on 29 November, a decision which we later realised was dictated by their fear of missing Christmas at home, they then spent the next three days going round the settlement telling everybody how marvellous the Expedition was and how much they had enjoyed the experience. Nelson was heard to observe that 'them boys works as good as Hislanders,' a comment which gave the Administrator the opportunity to indulge in a little mild sarcasm. Following the Tristan custom, when we had said our goodbyes to everybody on the road down to the harbour, Nelson and Andrew were on the quayside both with tears streaming down their faces and Richard and I found it difficult to talk to each other for the next twenty minutes. There is something dreadfully final about a departure from Tristan because one knows that one's chances of ever going there again are infinitesimal ...

CHAPTER 7

COOKING
The FASCINATION of WHAT is DIFFICULT

(This chapter is only of interest to people who are going to cook for lots of other people in primitive conditions.)

N.B.: If you do try eating the bird, make sure you spit out the beak. And, by the way, drumsticks on little birds don't have much meat on them.
P.S.: I am asked by the RSPB to remind you that by and large eating wild birds is WRONG.'

Bill Oddie: *The Little Black Bird Book*

As previously recorded, I had been given a list of all the equipment and food which was awaiting us in Cape Town for transhipment, together with another list of things to buy in Cape Town and later, from Tristan. My wife's disbelief in my ability to cook successfully for twelve people had so raised my ire, that I had given rather little consideration to these lists, (though I had already noted several appalling omissions) the more so that my view of the unprotected cargo on the wharfside in Cape Town had made me pray that our island guides would be very proficient not only in living off the land but also in teaching us to live therefrom. I lacked confidence in my supplies, nutritional or functional, though I was still determined to prove the inaccuracy of my wife's judgement. At least four-fifths of the promised supplies did eventually emerge from the mysterious black plastic bags once they had been identified and catalogued. The immediate problem when we had landed on 16 October was to feed people satisfactorily three times a day, not knowing either where the cookers were, nor how they worked, nor what each of the innumerable black plastic bags contained.

I knew that the diet on *Agulhas* had been so plentiful that all members of the Expedition could live on accumulated fat for at least four days but realised that some evidence of culinary efficiency would be appreciated within twenty-four hours, if only for the sake of morale. Nevertheless, Kendal Mint Cake had to serve as breakfast on the first morning after landing, as this was the only container which was readily available and identifiable. By lunchtime I had found cheese and biscuits among other commodities and in the afternoon one of the two-ring paraffin cookers had materialised (the other one never did!) I cooked some chicken noodle soup on one ring, and a tinned stew to which I added some French beans on the other, but the complication of keeping one saucepan hot while getting all the ingredients properly cooked for the second dish were considerable, particularly as the winds blew freely around the area where I was cooking and the instructions on the Valor cooker said clearly that it would not operate in any kind of draught! I had a grand total of two saucepans capable of dealing with the quantities involved in feeding twelve people, plus one large frying pan, and this necessitated a certain amount of jiggery pokery in the use of the smaller saucepans.

The programme for meals had been outlined to me by Michael in some ten minute interlude during the doom-laden twelve hours of briefing on 1 October:

Breakfast:	porridge, tea
Lunch:	beef tea or soup - light high energy foods - cheese, Kendal Mint Cake, chocolate, fruit when available.
Dinner:	main meal - tinned or dehydrated meat, potatoes, rice or pasta, dehydrated vegetables, supplement main course by living off the land, particularly by fishing (other sources of nourishment left vague). Pudding - cakes, whips, dehydrated fruit, fresh fruit as long as it would last, biscuits.

Generous supplies of tea, rather less so of coffee, plenty of fruit drinks.

We would have to collect an oven from Tristan which would

enable us to make bread from the plentiful supplies of flour of various varieties with which we had been endowed.

Having got through the first day, I ventured into the porridge department with tea on the second morning. Knowing very little about porridge (the only time when I had ever willingly eaten it was as a junior member of Woodard House, Denstone College, in the period 1950-52 - then, as now, starvation was the alternative) my first effort was a trifle salty but at least it taught me that the so-called controls on the cooker were as totally inadequate as I had suspected the previous evening and it taught the other members of the Expedition that all things were possible and even capable of improvement. On 17 October, while other members of the Expedition stood around watching whoever was on duty wielding the solitary pick, in order to clear a site of some fifty feet by twenty-five feet on a slope of one in ten, I settled down to cooking a lot of potatoes and then peeling them - they would be cold in the evening, but I could pour over them a boiling and life-giving meat/vegetable stew in sufficient quantities to heat them up and to provide a more satisfying basic meal so that my ravenous young entry could possibly even appreciate the taste of the rest of it. The lunch was soup and cheese and biscuits followed by chocolate bars.

Part of my entry in my diary on the evening of the 18th reads:

'By evening the site was two-thirds cleared - supper was much more of a success and I was able to eat some, thanks to a quick gulp of whisky beforehand - obviously my stomach is expecting alcohol before a meal and when it doesn't get it, I don't eat! Got supper on by 6.30, which made getting to bed less of a shambles and I was able to write up the Expedition Log by torchlight for the 16th.'

In the intervening time the problem had still been tracking down the multifarious missing items from the food list, as well as providing some kind of satisfactory and different meal in the evening, which was the big meal of the day and the one where it was important to have variety.

The difficulties of supplying a satisfying hot meal for twelve people with two paraffin-fired rings to cook on, became apparent even before we had moved into the hut, where the draught problems were at least generally excluded. The three dimensional proportions of the 'kitchen' were generous when related to the total volume of the hut and to the volume of the two store tents outside. [*See plate 9*]. True, the terminals of the wind generator were in the corner by the door giving on to the exterior, as were the large plastic refuse bags, and on the other side, the water carriers, but even so, there was space for two people to move freely within the cooking area, and this area I tried, somewhat jealously to preserve.

It is possible that the rest of this chapter is only of interest to basic cooks. Certainly it can be divided into different recipe headings, with particular emphasis on the party recipes given for 26 November!

Apart from the basic *Bee Nilson Penguin Cook Book* (which astonishingly contained not a single recipe for penguin), I had thought it appropriate to take Jocasta Innes' *Pauper's Cook Book* and this was of great utility despite two basic deficiencies of supply, one nutritional and one culinary. I don't know what is the proportion of recipes which require either onions or shallots but judging by the cookery books on Inaccessible, I would suspect that four out of five recipes for main courses require one or the other. We had neither, nor had we any powdered equivalent, and our supplies of powdered garlic amounted to two four-ounce tins. During our voyage on the *Agulhas* Chief Islander Albert had promised us bags of onions and an oven, together with our two guides. Grateful though we were for our two guides, it turned out that though their capacious baggage contained five bags of potatoes, there was nothing else for general consumption and what remained was their own private property. No onions, no oven. The lack of an oven - one which could be clapped on top of a paraffin ring, a kind which was readily available on Tristan - was to prove rather aggravating as there were so many simple recipes which could have added a little variety to the daily diet and by which I could have prepared dishes economically at the same time as the preparation of something basic, like the potatoes.

On 12 November, returning from a reasonably easy 'sched' at about 5.20 pm, the respective 'mates' of the botanist and the Invertebrate Zoologist met me as I sweated my way to the door.

"John, do you want the good news first or the bad news?"

Unthinking. "Give me the good news."

"Nelson and Andrew have killed two dozen shearwaters as well as collecting a lot of eggs."

"So what's the bad news?"

"The shearwaters are supper, and you're cooking them ..." [*See plate 10*].

On that first occasion, curry powder and the change of meat texture carried me through but by the time we had eaten curried shearwater for two successive evenings, I decided to experiment. I considered Miss Innes' instructions for Rabbit Marengo (4 helpings) as exemplified in *The Pauper's Cook Book*, Penguin Edition, pages 63-64. They read as follows:

'1 young rabbit cut into serving pieces, 3 tbsp olive oil, 1 small onion, 1 clove garlic, 1 tbsp chopped parsley, 1 tbsp tomato paste, ½ pint water, ¼lb mushrooms or mushroom stalks, salt, pepper, a small knob of butter, juice of ½ lemon.

'Heat olive oil in a large frying pan till it smokes. Fry the rabbit, turning the pieces frequently till browned all over. Transfer the rabbit to a dish in the oven to keep warm (gas 1, 250°F, 120°C) while you make the sauce. Put the oil in which the rabbit was cooked into a saucepan and stir in the finely chopped onion and garlic, parsley, tomato paste (tomato concentrate in a tube is best for this), butter and water. Mix well and simmer for a minute or two. Add sliced mushrooms to this sauce and cook till tender, stirring occasionally. Add lemon juice (or 1 tbsp wine vinegar), salt and pepper to taste, and pour the sauce over the rabbit pieces. Cover the dish and cook for 45 minutes in a moderate oven (gas 4, 350°F, 190°C).

'Serve with plain boiled rice, peas or beans.'

The ingredients, interpreted into Inaccessible language (12 helpings), read as follows:

'24 shearwater (assorted ages) cut into small serving pieces, vegetable cooking oil, powdered garlic, Cape 'Mixed Herbs,' half a 7lb tin of peeled tomatoes with juice, 4oz concentrated dehydrated mushroom soup, 1 pint water, salt, pepper, juice of two tired oranges, dehydrated sliced French beans.'

The reinterpretation of the instructions was as follows:

'I fried the shearwater meat with vegetable oil in two lots in the giant frying pan, transferring the meat when browned all over to a plastic bucket, and divided the oil equally between the two large saucepans. I added a liberal teaspoon of powdered garlic and a liberal dessertspoon of mixed herbs to each saucepan and then divided the peeled tomatoes between them, complete with juice. The addition of several dessertspoons of butter changed the consistency of the sauce, as did the 'mashing' of the tomatoes with the aid of a fork. From the kettle (which was always on one of the rings when they were not being used to cook something else) I poured a pint of hot water on to the four ounces of mushroom soup concentrate in a measuring jug and divided that between the two saucepans, adding salt, pepper and juice of one tired orange to each. Taking two saucepans off their rings (in case the contents burned), I threw several handfuls of dehydrated French beans into the small saucepan and added hot water until the beans had swelled out to their normal size. The contents of the plastic bucket were then divided between the two big saucepans which were returned to the rings for 'moderate' boiling. As the rings only produced heat at full blast, this meant constant stirring (I could have used one or two members of the Expedition for this task but they were rarely present at the requisite time) and a readiness to remove either saucepan from the cooker should the contents begin to boil over. The French beans were added about ten minutes before serving time and the 'Shearwater Marengo' was then poured over cold boiled potatoes.'

If there has been some emphasis on equal division in the preceding paragraph, the phrase became even more important at serving-time. The other plastic bucket, full of peeled boiled potatoes, was put beside the serving tea chest and I would announce the ration as the first clients rolled in, slavering. At first I used to say 'three potatoes,' but when it became apparent that this was not specific enough (excellent though the Tristan potatoes were, they were not all grown to the same size), I modified the instruction to 'Three potatoes, one large, one medium, one small.' The contents of one of the saucepans was then divided between the first six clients, hot stew being ladled over cold potatoes, and the same procedure repeated with the remaining saucepan and the other half of the Expedition.

The actual phrase in the prospectus of the Expedition concerning living off the land read, as far as I can recollect, 'We shall supplement our diet by fishing.'

We had equipped ourselves with fishing lines in Cape Town and had learnt the technique of fishing offshore as already recorded: the most highly valued piscatorial prize had been the species called Snoek, which looked like a cross between a barracuda and a mackerel and which had to be treated with extreme caution when landed as its jaws looked fully capable of unseaming anybody from the nave to the chaps with all the resultant unpleasant consequences. Neither the Snoek nor the Bluefish, however, came close inshore, and when Nelson and Andrew decided that the sea and the time were appropriate for fishing on Saturday, 23 October, (encouraged no doubt by a lentil stew the previous evening), apart from the odd Beva, it was the ubiquitous Five Finger which was the prey they had in mind. Shaped rather like a perch, the Five Finger ranges in size from a small sole to a smallish halibut, and takes its name from the five black vertical stripes which it bears on each side of its body.

The Skuas on West Point had been inclined to treat us with familiarity during the first week but Nelson, in search of bait, dispatched one with a deadly accurate stone and it was amazing how quickly the word seemed to spread among the Skuas: later, the unfortunate rockhoppers and petrels had far less chance of making their escape. Having baited their hooks and weighted their lines with carefully chosen, carefully tied stones, our guides would wait for the next big wave and, once it was committed, would hurl their lines over and beyond the advancing crest. It was then a question of waiting with the line raised high before the face and the finger tense on the line. It was not difficult to learn to distinguish between a bite and the pull of the backwash but it was more difficult to cast far enough without impaling one's leg or fingers in a whirling hook, and even more difficult to tie the stone-weight in such a way that one did not lose it as soon as some impediment blocked its withdrawal along the seabed. Nelson and Andrew seemed to lose a weight in about one cast out of five, but I found my average was more like three out of five. When the line refused to budge, the conventional reaction was to wind some line around one's waist, turn one's back on the sea and advance resolutely up the shingle until something broke. A prolonged period of rehooking, rebaiting or reweighting was then inclined to ensue.

Our guides always drew in their catches as fast as possible because it was very easy to lose a fish in the backwash or catch one in a tangle of rocks just at the sea's edge where it was dangerous to risk the attack of the next breaker. On good fishing days (as on 23 October) they would quickly build up a pile of fish and once the number got into double figures, Nelson would begin to 'fillet.' His method, whatever the size of the fish, was to cut from behind the back of the head diagonally down towards the bottom of the stomach and then slice a triangular piece of flesh from that side of the fish towards the tail, before turning it over and repeating the same procedure on the other side. All the rest of the fish was discarded which seemed to me a terrible waste, particularly with the larger specimens, so I set to work by myself. After some twenty minutes of concentrated effort, I produced two rectangular fillets which admittedly left far less of the fish for the marauding Skuas but which later proved more or less inedible because they were so full of bones!

The catch was so good on that first fishing day that even though I went on cooking fillets 'meunière' (regrettably with UNclarified butter) until everybody had had enough, there were still plenty of fillets left over. These I placed in one of the large saucepans with a generous sprinkling of Cape Herbs and pepper, covering with water which I allowed to simmer for ten minutes before setting the saucepan aside with a lid on until the following day.

Miss Nilson's recipe for Fish Pie is on page 120 of the *Penguin Cookery Book* and runs as follows:

1½lb hot mashed potato, ½ pint cheese sauce or parsley sauce, 6-8 tbsp milk, salt, pepper, margarine or dripping. 1lb boiled fish, flaked.

Mash the potato and milk until creamy, seasoning well. Line a pie dish with a third of it. Mix the fish and sauce and season well. Pour into the dish and cover with the remaining potato. Dot the top with margarine or dripping and bake in a hot oven until brown on top and heated through.

In Inaccessiblese, this ran something like this:

800 gm of a large box of dehydrated mashed potato, ½ pint milk (made from powder), salt, pepper, powdered nutmeg, several lbs of boiled Five Finger, all bones removed, flaked, 2 pints cheese sauce (no question of parsley sauce, no parsley), margarine.

The cheese sauce was made by the usual 'roux' method with the water from the boiled fish as stock. Our supplies of huge blocks of Cheddar cheese were inclined to liquefy in their plastic wrapping but they lasted well and were our staple lunch diet for eight weeks apart from the few days when eggs were available. Grating about a pound of it without a grater involved chopping it as fine as possible with one of the big kitchen knives and then mashing the crumbs with a fork and the fingers. The cheese sauce, once made, was added to the flaked fish and I turned my attention to the mashed potato. The powder was placed at the bottom of a plastic bucket and boiling water added in exactly the right proportion. Milk, butter and nutmeg were then added, together with the fish in the cheese sauce, and the whole mixture was vigorously whisked. Not only was this both tasty and filling but it was one of the few recipes in which all the ingredients could be served hot.

It is no accident that the first three 'Inaccessible' recipes in this book all originated from fresh sources rather than from dehydrated or tinned supplies. Both the latter proved adequate (and were, in fact, much easier to prepare) but it was very difficult to distinguish dehydrated mutton from dehydrated chicken (the latter came eventually to be designated 'chicken pellets' whenever my efforts had failed to disguise it sufficiently and such efforts inevitably produced excessive inroads into the curry and spice stocks). A well-known firm had supplied us with several boxes of their various tinned meat products: 'Steak with gravy,' 'Steak with onions and gravy,' and 'Steak pie with mushrooms.' The two former products were excellent in providing the meat/vegetable stew mentioned before, which could reheat the potatoes but the clientèle soon became bored if they were produced too often and anyway if stocks were to last until Christmas and beyond, their use had to be curtailed.

The 'Steak pie with mushrooms' included pastry. Perhaps I should rephrase that sentence. The large flat tins ('a meal for two persons') contained a thick flabby slice of pastry which occupied over three-quarters of the tin and which might well have proved extremely filling had we been able to cook it. As it was, I was reduced to using the remaining quarter of the tin which consisted of two mushrooms, three bits of 'steak' (provenance uncertain) and gravy. Even allowing one tin per person, the 'Steak pie with mushrooms' provoked outraged protest on the two occasions when it appeared on the menu.

The superiority of our own product was again evident once we started to cook our own bread. Nick had put a great deal of thought into this and was more frustrated than anybody when the promised oven failed to materialise. As it was perfectly clear that the cream crackers which formed our staple lunch for the first week would only last another six days if consumed at the same rate, pending the construction of an oven, Nick produced a Chapatti recipe, also known as Soda Bread. This made a satisfactorily agreeable filler for the starving young (who joined enthusiastically in its production) and I therefore include the recipe for anybody unfortunate enough to be caught in similar circumstances:

(For twelve, two Chapattis per person)

1½ lbs stonemeal flour, 1½ oz baking powder, ½ teasp salt.

Mix dry, very thoroughly. Put two handfuls (per person) into another mixing bowl. Add 2 fl oz water - mix well but do not knead. Throw into a pan containing covering of oil: cook for five to ten minutes, two at a time.

The disadvantage of the Chapattis was that their preparation was very time consuming and when Joe announced his intention of making an earth oven in front of the hut, I assumed that all our bread making problems were over, such was my faith in his ingenuity. In fact, the earth oven was the only occasion when it failed and it was Ian who finally invented the patent Inaccessible oven which he improvised out of an empty paraffin tin and which was heated by the two small Primuses originally sent for use when camping on top of the island. This produced excellent bread and cakes, particularly when Dick was responsible for the kneading of the dough; he was not merely a scientist but a perfectionist.

Nelson and Andrew, as mentioned previously, had arrived with fairly capacious luggage quite apart from the precious bags of potatoes. The contents of this luggage were not immediately apparent until it emerged that Andrew's birthday fell on 27 November, and I was approached by every member of the Expedition individually (apart from Nelson and Andrew), each wishing to make it clear that a special gastronomic effort was required for this occasion. Three of the courses needed little or no preparation. The first was grapefruit juice, several tins of which I had hoarded even after the supply of fresh oranges was exhausted. Similarly, having consulted my co-leader, we had decided that we would sacrifice the Christmas puddings and the Christmas cake, the former prepared by Sarah Hall and the latter by Elizabeth Swales, many months earlier in England, and pray that the Expedition was safely on Tristan for Christmas as per plan and per invitation. That left the entremet and the main course. I would have liked to present Filets de Cinq Doigts Meunière as the entremet but had too much experience of the weather to trust that the 27th would be a fishing day. (In fact, there was no fishing at all between the 18 and 29 November, the day when the Tristan launches finally arrived to take the first five of us back to Tristan.)

Even though the main course was to be Shearwater Marengo, a well-tried favourite, I decided to make Shearwater Pâté as a precaution on the 26th, basing myself on Miss Innes' recipe for Rabbit Pâté, which runs as follows:

1 rabbit, weighing approx. 1 lb, 1 lb belly pork, ½lb fatty bacon rashers, 10 juniper berries, thyme, parsley, 3 cloves garlic, a pinch of mace, 1 teasp grated lemon peel, 2 tbsp cider, white wine or sherry, bay leaves.

Ask the butcher to cut the rabbit into pieces. Simmer these in a little water for 25 minutes. Leave to cool. Remove all the flesh from the bones and chop, or mince, it together with the pork (from which you have removed any rind and bone), garlic, and a generous handful of thyme and parsley, and the juniper berries. A mincer saves time, but diligent chopping with a sharp knife gives better results. Season the mixture with quite a lot of black pepper, pinch of mace, grated lemon rind, and a pinch of salt. Add the cider, wine or sherry. If you are not in a hurry, leave the ingredients to stand for 1-2 hours to mix the flavours well. Line the bottom and sides of a medium sized mixing bowl, or of 2 smaller earthenware oven dishes, with the rashers of bacon, rinds removed. Pack in the ingredients. Lay 2 bay leaves on top and cover with more bacon rashers. Cover the bowl or dishes with a lid, foil or plate. Cook standing in a pan with a little water in it, in a slowish oven (gas 3, 325°F, 160°C) for about two hours or until the pâté starts coming away from the sides of the container. The cooking time will be longer in one large container than in two smaller ones. Remove from oven. Lay a sheet of greaseproof paper on top, weight it, and leave overnight. If you are not planning to eat it at once seal the pâté by pouring over a little melted lard.

Three quarters of the ingredients were lacking, and for 'Rabbit' read 'Shearwater;' the reinterpretation then runs something like this:

Take 20 shearwaters and extract the flesh. Just as our guides knew the quickest way of filleting Five Fingers, they wasted no time on the shearwaters, cutting out the two sides of the breastbone and the two drumsticks and discarding the rest without hesitation. The normal practice then was to chop each piece of meat into two or three sections and these sections were duly 'simmered' for twenty-five minutes and left to cool, before attacking them again with the kitchen knife to reduce them to the requisite minimal size for 'pâté.' The other ingredients consisted of a lot of butter, Cape mixed herbs, powdered garlic, pepper, salt and brandy. As we had little or no excuse for employing the Expedition brandy for medicinal reasons, Nick and I had some pleasure in employing it for culinary purposes, both in the pâté and in the brandy butter which was to accompany the Christmas pudding. Three of the porridge tins (which had plastic tops and were excellent for storage, picnics and, in this case, cooking) fitted exactly into one of the large saucepans, so having left the mixture to stand for a couple of hours, I packed each porridge tin to the top, put weights on the plastic lids and simmered them over a 'low' primus with a 'little' water for the requisite two hours, being a little upset half-way through the process to discover that melted butter was bubbling over and pouring down the sides of each tin. Luckily I had been more than generous in the amount I had used and anyway I was able to compensate by sealing each tin with more butter once the cooking was over. Then I hid the tins by putting them back with the unopened ones.

All this took some time and I have forgotten what we ate for the main meal that night but it must have been something fairly simple. We did a lot of signing envelopes and stamping because the wind had changed and there was a feeling that just possibly the barge might be coming for Andrew's birthday, though we knew it was unlikely and once we saw the swell the following morning, we knew there was no chance.

It was, however, fine and while half the Expedition took advantage of this unexpected bonus to go to the top, I cast caution to the absent winds and cooked as many potatoes as I could fit into the two big saucepans. As there were very few for lunch, I decided to try out the 'pâté' by using half a tin. The speed at which it disappeared was reassuring.

Everybody was busy in the afternoon. Personally I went ringing shearwaters on the precipice behind the hut with Nelson,

Andrew and Mike, before coming down alone in order to go up to the top for the 'sched' with Ian. I think that was the day when Ian achieved the record thirty-four minute ascent: I was well satisfied with my own forty-nine minutes but by the time I had got back and had got the Shearwater Marengo under way, there was a suppressed air of excitement in the hut as more people straggled in, more people started appearing in jackets and ties (!) and Andrew's mysterious baggage was revealed to be something like the contents of the average cocktail cabinet, accompanied by vast quantities of beer.

It was a very jolly evening and I can remember nearly all of it, but my abiding memory is of the sheer quantity of (very rich) food which disappeared down eleven throats (Gilfie was unable to participate because of a stomach complaint and must have felt very frustrated). Everything edible vanished, and as the quantity of food available was at least three times the normal ration, this is some measure of the restraint which had been exercised as normal procedure in the previous six weeks, particularly by the hungry young.

Perhaps three extracts from my diary sum up the basic monotony of the situation, if not from the point of view of the consumer, at least from the point of view of the cook. On 14 November, I wrote:

'One of the things that slows life down is the fact that every drop of water has to be carried over a hundred yards, every pint of milk has to be made from powder, every five hours the paraffin has to be filled up in the Tilly lamps. No electric light because the wind generator isn't powerful enough. No heat, so if things get wet, we have to wait for the sun to dry them.'

On 1 November, there are two extracts: the first reads:

'I know why Sylvie gets so angry when I ask her What's for dinner three or four hours in advance - cooking for twelve is a very salutary experience!'

The second reads:

'After this trip, all members of the Expedition are going to have to come and stay with us in Yorkshire, if only to prove that, given proper equipment, I CAN cook!'

CHAPTER 8

BIRDS

> .... *My heart in hiding*
> *Stirred for a bird, - the achieve of,*
> *the mastery of the thing!*
> G. M. Hopkins: *The Windhover*

Three-quarters of an hour out of Cape Town, with the helicopter hardly safely on board, the first couple of Cape Pigeon appeared, their unmistakable piebald colouration making them instantly recognisable and the suggestion of slight variations in their colouration being perhaps responsible for the common nomenclature which associates them with the even greater variation in the feral pigeon. I quickly learned from the professional ornithologists to call them Pintados, and this new found piece of learning was of almost immediate use following my return to the classroom in January, when I was able to explain that 'scared Cape Pigeon' in a poem about Cape Horn were, in fact, Pintado Petrels and were almost certainly not 'scared.' The 5th form was suitably impressed but what impressed me about the Pintado was that I never once saw one from land, either from Inaccessible or Tristan, nor, as far as I know, did we ever catch one which had been dazzled or attracted by the lights of either of the ships on which I sailed. Nevertheless, once the ship was sailing, the Pintados appeared, usually a couple but sometimes more, and remained more or less omnipresent throughout the voyage, disappearing mysteriously about half an hour before one reached port.

I have watched birds in an amateur sort of fashion from a very early age and birds were my greatest source of pleasure during the Expedition, particularly once I had learned to identify the basic species of the South Atlantic without difficulty, a process which was largely accomplished during the ten-day voyage of the *Agulhas*. Our ornithologist, Mike, had been delighted to find that four South African ornithologists from the Percy Fitzpatrick Institute of the University of Cape Town were travelling to Gough Island on the *Agulhas* and they were of great assistance to him, though in far too expert a class for me. Nevertheless, when bird-watching started in earnest on the helicopter deck after dinner on the first evening, even the experts were 'twitching' when a White-capped (or 'Shy') Albatross was spotted. For me, at that stage, it was an albatross. Similarly, the White-chinned Petrel which also appeared that evening was to me a petrel; rather a large one compared with the very few British storm-petrels I had encountered in the North Sea and not bearing much resemblance to our Fulmar but a species with which I was to become very familiar in its 'Spectacled Shoemaker' form on Inaccessible.

There was a considerable sea running as the light began to fade and one had to learn to adapt to the heave of the stern while keeping the bird one was trying to observe in view, sometimes hanging on to a convenient piece of ship with the hand which was not holding the binoculars. I had brought a safety harness for my spectacles and this came in very useful because it enabled me to push the spectacles aside quite quickly when I wanted to use my field glasses, but it was several days before I learned to follow the wave-skimming birds with any kind of success and I didn't really become aware of the existence of prions until I was able to look down on them from the much greater height of the bridge, when I was supposedly keeping watch on the third day of the voyage. In the intervening period, I spent a considerable time on the helicopter deck, a desolate sort of place in the grey light of the early morning and particularly desolate on the first morning when most members of the Expedition were too seasick or too tired to venture forth and only Mike and I and one UCT man (THEY had a rota) were present.

This gave Mike the chance to teach me why the albatross we could see was a Black-browed Albatross and not some other variety but it was a lesson which did not really sink home until recollected in tranquillity some considerable time later. The fact that it did sink home is borne out by my positive identification of a Grey-headed Albatross on the first day of our voyage back to Cape Town on *Tristania II* (two months later, almost to the day) and I felt considerable pride in being able to do so. Whether I also felt a 'twitcher's' pride in being able to add the Grey-headed Albatross to my list is more debateable ... (there is a note in my diary for 10 October which reads: 'The ornithologists have all drunk too much this evening because they saw a Grey-headed Albatross.')

Why does it matter that one should see a Grey-headed Albatross and how important is it that one should be able to identify it correctly? There is a certain snobbery among bird-watchers which has been, if anything, intensified by Bill Oddie's *Little Black Bird Book,* vastly amusing though I find that erudite work, and I had better make it clear that in my own mind I classify bird-watchers into three main groups.

There are first the 'pure scientists,' who painstakingly measure and record the size of the egg, the length of the wing, the number of times the hen leaves the nest to feed and all the minutiae; (these people are prepared to put up with foul conditions and work extremely long hours in the course of their investigations.)

Secondly the 'twitchers,' who race around not just all over their own country but frequently all over the world, in order to add a rare bird to their list. The *Little Black Bird Book* describes them fairly comprehensively, both their foibles and their virtues, and it is only fair to say that the best of them are prepared to put up with pretty foul conditions too. There is a certain conflict between the 'ringing' scientists and the 'twitchers,' because ringing a rare bird, or ringing a bird in a place where it is not supposed to be found is apt to make it clear off, thus giving the 'twitcher' less chance to make an addition to his list!

Both the first two groups are inclined to regard the third group of bird-watcher (to which I attach myself) with scorn, amusement, indignation or, exceptionally and as exemplified in both our Michaels (the one who couldn't lead us and the one who joined us at the last moment), with a tolerance of our ignorance and with an ability to communicate the maximum amount of information which they judged we were able to digest at a given moment. This third group does not make its living from ornithology (vide Captain Leith in Chapter 3 on this subject), nor has it the time nor the money to 'twitch:' it merely takes pleasure in observing birds when it has the chance, and few 'third-groupers' can have had a greater chance than I. I write the rest of this chapter from my own position in the third group, so let no scientific ornithologist nor 'twitcher' imagine that what follows represents the results of the Expedition's research.

The 'indolents compagnons de voyage' swung effortlessly around the stern of the *Agulhas* and by lunchtime on that first full day at sea, when the swell had calmed down considerably, two great Wanderers had been identified. The albatross has been described by Colonel van der Post as 'the greatest white hunter and slayer of vast distances in this world.' It seems impossible to capture the sheer majesty of the Wandering Albatross in the air, either in words or even on film; they hung apparently motionless beside one as the *Agulhas* forged along at fourteen knots, glancing ever so slightly sidewards and downwards at the puny mortals desperately focusing their field glasses and their cameras, a look on their faces which reminded me very forcibly of something I had read long ago about the visage of Louis XIV.

Very different was the expression on the face of the Giant Petrel which also appeared on that first day to squabble over the scraps thrown from the galley: rapacious, blood-thirsty and apparently thoroughly deserving of their 'Stinker' (Tristan) patronymic, there was yet something clumsy about their bodies on the water and something innocent when they were at rest which made me wonder if this was where Tenniel found his model for the Dodo in *Alice*.

I don't know why bird-watching from the bridge was so different from bird-watching from the helicopter deck at the stern. There was of course a big difference in altitude but there was more to it than that. In the first place, on the bridge one was keeping watch and could not therefore make it too obvious that one was bird-watching, particularly if Captain Leith was marching up and down in quick-time behind one's back. The vastness of the ocean and the depths beneath one's feet seemed infinitely greater from the bridge than they did from the stern, possibly because on the helicopter deck one had before one the whole reassuring bulk of the *Agulhas* with its life and amenities to blunt the emptiness of the grey wastes of ocean. The larger birds, the albatrosses, shearwaters and petrels, seemed to frequent the stern whereas from the bridge, on 8 October, I saw considerable flocks of prions and terns and, to my delight, a storm-petrel scuttering delicately across the waves on the starboard side. I was even more delighted to identify it later as a Wilson's Storm-petrel, which bears the mind-boggling name *Oceanites oceanicus* and which together with the Great and Sooty Shearwater, is one of the three species which breed in the Southern Hemisphere but which cross the equator in large numbers to 'winter.' There is something even more impressive about this minute bird, sometimes solitary and usually only in groups of two or three, making that enormous journey than there is about the much larger shearwater migrating in millions, even though the Great Shearwater's feat in finding the tiny islets of Nightingale and Inaccessible is something on which the Captain of *Tristania II* might well find time to reflect!

As the voyage progressed and the sea, amazingly, grew calmer, I became more blasé about new sightings. The 9 October was my day for the three shearwaters, the Great, the Little and the Sooty, but it stays more in my mind for the advice given by a member of the UCT ornithological team on how to recognise a Kerguelen Petrel: 'It's like an Afrikaner - the forehead is the largest part of its face!' The closer we came to Gough, the more the bird population increased and the more I could still marvel at the unforgettable sight of four or five albatrosses planing over our wake. The 10 October, the day of the Grey-headed Albatross, which I didn't see, was also the day of the first Yellow-nosed, which I did, and the 11th, the day of our arrival at Gough, was the day which opened our eyes to the ornithological experiences which were yet to unroll before us in cornucopian profusion.

Fog, rain, wind and swell arrived in fairly equal proportions and by midday Captain Leith had given permission for fishing to take place (though he did not finally abandon hope of flying the helicopter until 6.30 pm). By that time, the sea to the east was dotted with huge rafts of prions and once it became dark, they and a variety of petrels and storm-petrels were attracted by the lights of the ship and began to accumulate in all sorts of strange places on board (one even came through the window into the bar, but it is suspected that an anti-ornithologist had a hand in that event). The prions were in the greatest numbers and were the easiest to catch and also the most difficult to relaunch [*See plate 11*]; one of them sat on my head for at least five minutes without showing any desire to depart, and several, when relaunched by hand, were seen to turn round and come straight back to the ship. Even the bird books are cagy about identifying the different species of prion because the only feature which distinguishes them is the breadth and proportion of their bills and the instruction in one of our Guides said simply that sightings at sea should be catalogued as 'Prions' with no attempt to particularise. The variety we captured was invariably the Broad-billed Prion and it was very obvious why the old whalers used to call it the 'Fire-bird,' the name coming from its habit of being attracted to and flying into fires at night.

Much more delicate were the storm-petrels which came on board in quite considerable numbers, particularly the White-faced species, but also the White-bellied and the Grey-backed, of which latter Mike wrote in the official Log: 'but no. 1 for me so far are the Grey-backed Storm-petrel, exquisite little beasts, delicately patterned and so fragile-looking, definitely ephemeral.' [*See plate 12*].

Quite often we only discovered overnight visitors the following morning and then one had to leave them in their hiding place and hope they would survive the day, because relaunching them during daylight hours was more or less offering a free meal to a passing Skua. On 12 October, the poop-deck was a gory shambles by 6.45 am, with dying fish littered all over the place, fishermen shouting and hauling lines, non-fishermen getting in the way and, in the middle of it all was

Mike, looking behind capstans, sticking his nose into every possible cranny, wildly excited by the number of birds he had been able to handle and identify since the previous evening: I have a sneaking suspicion that he was up all night. By that time his list extended to thirty-four species, which is some measure of his tribute to the Grey-backed Storm-petrel.

The most interesting ornithological observation during our first, luckily abortive, trip to Inaccessible on 15 October occurred when we had anchored off Waterfall Beach in the evening and saw rafts of Great Shearwater on the sea to the north [*See Plate 13*]: the significance of the observation did not dawn on us (it may have done on Mike) until much later, in fact until 12 November, which was the first day when we noted (I quote my diary) 'great masses of shearwater wheeling in the sky.' It was the following day that Nelson and Andrew brought me the first seven shearwater eggs and this bears out the suggestion of Fisher and Lockley in 'Seabirds' (1954) that the more adult birds frequently arrive at their breeding sites some considerable time before nesting begins but for some reason do not venture ashore. Is it possible that they are reconnoitring the best fishing sites in order not to waste time once nesting has begun?

I have already recounted our desperate scramble along the Blenden Hall foreshore following our landing: the only birds I had time to observe on that occasion were the Great Skuas and that was because they were so unused to the human presence that one had practically to kick them out of the way in order to place one's foot on the next stone. Three of the four endemic land birds were immediately evident the following day: the ubiquitous and fearless Tristan Thrush, otherwise known as a Starchy, which looks very like its European counterpart but seemed to me more carnivorous: the Tristan Bunting, again bearing a distinct resemblance to the European Corn Bunting, though the male is more brightly coloured, which announced its presence by perching inquisitively on the storage tent as we tried to piece it together; finally, the omnipresent but invisible Inaccessible Flightless Rail whose 'cheep cheep cheep' in the depths of the tussock was a constant source of entertainment for the next month and indeed longer, because our interest never ceased, even after occasional captures. It is strange that so secretive and inconspicuous a bird should exist side by side with the Starchy, which was photographed on my bunk in the hut where it had freely entered, with the buntings which would perch beside us within touching distance, and with the Brown Noddies and albatrosses which did not leave their nests when a camera was poked to within six inches of their heads. There is little doubt that the Rails are preyed upon by at least two other species but their evasive tactics are certainly very successful because they are to be found in considerable numbers all over the island from the tussock on the shore right up to the summit. At first their cheeping would lure us to follow them deeper into the undergrowth, a vain procedure as there was no possibility of our progressing silently, and it soon became clear to us that we were being mocked. We therefore adopted the more correct ornithological strategy of sitting still in a likely spot and waiting, 'retenant notre haleine.' Having done this for an hour and a half in the early afternoon of 23 October, with cheeping noises coming from all directions but never a sight of a Rail, even Mike had had enough, and we split up, I deciding to take a walk along the shingle in the direction of the penguin rookeries. Stumbling along beyond the 'wash-house,' I heard the familiar noise in the tussock to my right and noticed a knee-high gap, through which I poked my head, advancing cautiously on all fours. Several smaller alleyways split off from the main one and there were cheeping noises from at least three directions so I settled down for another vigil, making myself as comfortable as possible. Approximately three minutes later, looking down one of the smaller tunnels about head-high on my right, I became aware of the silent approach of a dumpy little brown bird with a red eye and what looked like a mauvish sort of bib. He (or she) looked straight at me and I, immobile, gazed back. He cocked his head to one side and scuttled delicately down an even smaller alleyway, his 'cheep cheep cheep' echoing in my ears as I wished that I had brought my camera and had had it in position. On a later occasion, I sat for an hour and a quarter in the same place with the camera at the ready and never saw a feather.

By this time, of course, several sightings had been recorded and the next step was to achieve the capture of a live Rail, for which feat Mike was offering enormous rewards (twelve cans of beer or two large bars of chocolate!) though he himself was hard at work on the same project. Several of the younger members were encouraged to spend a considerable time attempting a capture during the next week and we all became secretive about the methods we were employing.

The mist-net ingeniously laid at ground level between the tussock stalks turned out to be a failure because the Rails unsportingly took advantage of the unlevel nature of the terrain to slip underneath it. The wrecked crayfish trap found among the flotsam, on which Mike and Nelson lavished tremendous komvosological care, looked very promising, particularly as the prey was offered a three-choice menu (which was certainly two more choices than any member of the Expedition ever got), until the day came when Mike arrived back at the hut from a bunting watch beside the Rail trap, his blood pressure spraying out of his ears. He had seen a Rail enter the trap, had reached down to pick it up, and the Rail had made a snappy exit through the side wall.

My own first effort involved a poacher's trick which I had learnt in my youth, with the usual Inaccessible modifications. The original trick was to put grain in a place where pheasants were known to foregather for several nights in succession, so that the word got round among the pheasant community: one had to be fairly selective about one's choice of site because otherwise word got round to the peasant community and thence to the keeper as well, so that on the fifth or sixth night, when the grain you put out had been soaked in whisky for the previous twenty-four hours, all you picked up the following morning was a good belting from the keeper instead of the half-dozen comatose fat pheasants that you had been expecting ... In Inaccessiblese, for 'grain' read 'porridge oats' and for 'whisky' read 'Cape brandy' (and even that was a sacrifice), but it turned out that the Inaccessible Rail was not partial to porridge oats (an aversion which I shared) and seemed to have teetotal tendencies which to me are distinctly foreign.

I went even further back into my childhood and devised a Cunning Trap on the well-known Government-approved Pooh method of catching Heffalumps. The next time a seven pound tomato tin was empty, I put it aside, having cut out the lid completely, and later proceeded down to my Rail-viewing complex, the tomato tin concealed amongst the load of refuse of which I was disposing, and Nick's botanical trowel concealed somewhere in my trousers. I dug a suitable hole at the junction of several alleyways, levelled up the rim of the tomato tin with the surrounding soil and placed a carefully disguised raft of twigs, leaves, tussock stalks and soil across the top. It must have been a good strong raft because absolutely nothing happened for the next forty-eight hours except, I suppose, that the Rail walked across it. I replaced the raft with three twigs and four blades of tussock and the trap looked about as Cunning as the original Pooh trap but it worked splendidly because the next time I went to visit it, the three twigs and four blades of tussock were lying in the bottom of the tin: the only trouble was that the Rail which had fallen in with them had clearly grown bored with his surroundings and had jumped out!

Gradually our enthusiasm began to wane, and as our guides seemed to have no Island-lore which extended to Rail-catching, our activities became restricted to recording near-misses. Somewhere near the summit, on the day when we had all made our first ascent, Joe had electrified the descending explorers by announcing that he had seen "something like a mouse or a vole" running through the undergrowth. This really would have hit the scientific headlines but an exhaustive search had produced nothing whatsoever and the occasion had faded from my mind when, on 10 November, I began an ascent with Gilfie at about quarter to three to do the 'sched.' We had not quite reached the end of the tussock but we knew we were making good time when I heard a loud "cheep cheep cheep" and saw the by now familiar small dark form scuttling across our path, closely followed by two mouse-like creatures. I plunged recklessly into the tussock to my left, missing the adult by inches but eventually catching one of the chicks, who was covered in sooty black down and who cheeped with such volume that I realised how many times we must have been hearing chicks when we thought we were pursuing adults. The next problem was what to do with him. There was no point in dashing back to the hut because Mike was somewhere up on top, so I placed our capture, still cheeping energetically, in the pocket of my anorak, being careful to leave a corner open so that he had plenty of air. We then continued to climb as fast as we could, but as we climbed, the cheeps grew fainter and fainter and it was with regret that I extracted a moribund chick from my pocket some five minutes short of the top. The scientists all told me that I had done the right thing and I think Egbert has been preserved in some bottle but I still feel like a murderer, a feeling which never occurred to me when anything was killed for food.

In view of Egbert's extreme youth, I did not feel justified in claiming the reward for the capture of a live Rail and anyway, by the time he got to Mike, the chick was as dead as John Cleese's parrot: nevertheless we indulged in a mild celebration in the course of that evening. The eventual first capture of a live Rail was achieved by Mike himself, almost accidentally, some considerable time later, also with his hands. The event (and the captive) was much photographed, much celebrated and will no doubt lead to important scientific conclusions. My own scientific conclusion is that the best equipment for catching Inaccessible Rails is bare hands.

The Rails, the Starchies, the buntings and, to a slightly lesser extent, the larger petrels and the Great Shearwaters, were more or less omnipresent all over the island, but the other species could be classified by altitude.

There were two Rockhopper Penguin rookeries on Blenden Hall, both to the north and one so close that we could hear raucous cries at all times when they were not drowned by the breakers or the wind. The Rockhoppers rapidly became a useful safety valve for at least half the Expedition when things became too claustrophobic. One could sit somewhere near the tussock-line in the middle of the rookery and watch the coming and going, remarking particularly the patience of those birds who were trying to land and who would miss their chance time and time again as a contrary current swept them back. They usually made it at about the eleventh attempt but sometimes they would be swept three or four hundred yards to the south and would then hopefully land if a suitable wave presented itself: they would then hop myopically from rock to rock, looking for home. Others, who were going fishing, had much less trouble because once they had chosen their moment, all they had to do was to dive beneath the advancing breaker at the critical moment and emerge triumphantly on the seaward side. The mortality was high and I never walked along the shingle without meeting at least one and normally several dying penguin, usually because they had caught a foot between the rocks which they were unable to extract, thus making themselves prey for patrolling Skuas. They were very vulnerable to man, even though they would hop energetically towards the sea or the tussock as one approached, except for the ones who were sleeping in the sun. A polite "Good morning" (or afternoon) in their ear would produce an immediate and indignant hop-off, but these were the ones who were plundered indiscriminately by our two guides when they needed fishing bait and, unlike the Skuas, the penguins seemed not only incapable of evasive action, but incapable of getting the message. I only ventured twice into the labyrinth of the rookery but even now when I sniff the sleeve of my anorak, I have a Proustian recollection of Inaccessible Island.

At about the same level as the Rockhopper rookery was the Skua bog, the haunt of those brown aerial pirates who filled the niche of our own Carrion Crow in the Inaccessible ecology but whose predatory capacities were much more developed and whose aerobatic skills in picking off the unwary prion could only awake one's unwilling admiration. It was more with fear than with admiration that one approached a Skua nest because the attack of both male and female showed the same propensity as the Snoek to unseam one from the nave to the chaps with the added possibility that he (or she) might then set your head upon his (or her) battlements. Numerous pictures exist of our heroic ornithologist avoiding this danger, but the first time it happened to Joe when he was trying to make a map on top of the island (the Skuas nested there too), he was distinctly miffed because nobody had warned him of the dangers. The Wilkin's Bunting survived in the *Phylica* trees surrounding the Skua bog despite the presence of the Skuas. but the fourth endemic land species was not immediately apparent to us and must wait its chronological turn.

Once the Great Shearwaters arrived, their nesting burrows were at the same level or just above the Rockhoppers and though they were inclined to nest in colonies, such were their numbers that they were to be found in most parts of the island and eggs were found lying out in the open, such was the pressure on burrow space. Nelson was greatly astonished by the increase in the shearwater population as his memory of previous (short) visits to Inaccessible was of two rather small colonies. The islanders were accustomed to 'harvesting' the shearwaters on Nightingale and the new profusion on Inaccessible put a gleam into Nelson's eye. a gleam which he and Andrew translated into action when they thought that the Tristan barge might be attempting a crossing, as they quickly collected two large paraffin tins of 'haigs' to send back to their wives. We were much more aware of the birds living around us at hut level during the first five nights on the island when we were in tents: apart from the Broad-billed prions. which seemed to share burrows with the shearwaters. there were a few White-chinned Petrels, but the commonest variety was the Soft-plumaged Petrel, whose call greatly resembled the first part of a curlew's, so that on two occasions I went to sleep imagining that I was camping on the Yorkshire moors (those of course were the two nights of rainstorms). Smaller than the Fulmar and quite considerably smaller than the White-chinned Petrel. the plumage is a pleasing sub-fusc mixture of greys and browns with only the underbelly actually white: it is a well-disguised bird which is surprisingly difficult to pick out if it is sitting motionless on the ground, though it made no effort to evade capture once caught in the torch's beam [*See Plate 14*].

The Tern has always appealed to me as an elegant species. elegant both in its appearance and in its deadly efficiency when

Author with friend.

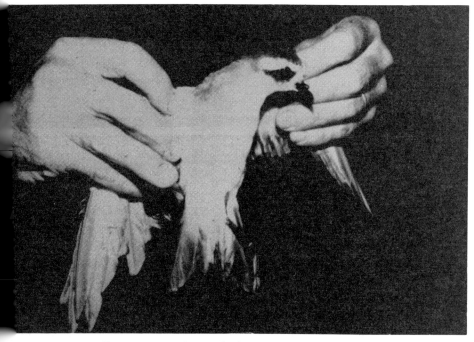

Storm-petrel, probably not Greybacked

Rafts of Great Shearwater off Inaccessible

Prion and Soft-Plumaged Petrel after ringing.

fishing, though its manners on the perching and nesting site seem to leave something to be desired. The Antarctic Terns which assembled on Tern Rock were indistinguishable from their Arctic brethren, living on various cliff sites just above the upper tussock line. To make the acquaintance of the biggest member of the family, the Brown Noddy, of which two or three pairs were nesting near the apples trees just before the first steep part of West Road, was an added pleasure because apart from their tameness, they seemed to have such good manners. As the species are not supposed to range more than fifty miles from land, this must have been an indigenous Tristan group colony. They took no exception to being photographed at close range and even took some interest in our own proceedings. There was the afternoon when I joined the botanist and the Invertebrate Zoologist who were both grubbing about enthusiastically under the apple trees: having got over my initial astonishment that last year's fruit was lying on the ground rotting while this year's blossom fell on it, I became aware of a presence immediately above my head. I was face to face with a Brown Noddy who had arrived quite silently and who was now regarding the proceedings of the scientists, his blue eyes cocked ever so slightly to one side, with the same benevolent interest that I had accorded them some quarter of an hour previously. An eminently gentle, family-loving bird, it is appropriate that its Tristan name is Wood Pigeon! I suppose they gained an added distinction because they were so few in number: the same was true of the Sooty Albatross, whom we encountered in a nesting-site of three on the second steep stretch of West Road. The dark colouring of both these birds seems to give an added intelligence to their faces but there is something even more haunting about the latter, something which made the old sailors believe that the souls of dead shipmates were reincarnated in this bird. One wonders where the sailors could have heard that wailing howl which echoed from the cliffs of Inaccessible because I never heard it at sea, which has induced the islanders to call them 'Pioos,' a name which I found totally inadequate to convey the full despair of the cry. Most people are not aware that it is this bird which hung around the neck of the Ancient Mariner and presumably picture some large species of white gull in that position [*See Plate 7*]. It is interesting that I have no recollection of seeing a Sooty Albatross in the twenty-odd days I was at sea, though the birds in the three nests on the route up to the top became very familiar because they were a regular stopping-point for a breather and they were as little camera conscious as were the Yellow-nosed variety, who were scattered in large numbers all over the main area of the island, four hundred metres above our hut.

These latter were the centre of attraction, or rather one was, on 24 October, the day when the whole Expedition made the first (and last) joint ascent. It was, to say the least of it, a somewhat straggling ascent but when we finally arrived en haut, minus the Invertebrate Zoologist still grubbing about a hundred metres down, the particular Yellow-nosed Albatross which happened to be sitting the nearest to the cliff edge very quickly became the most photographed Yellow-nosed Albatross in history. We recorded many 'Mollys' on that day (to use their Tristan name): their only sign of alarm when one came very close was to make a clicking noise with their beaks as they sat stolidly on their stalks of earth and fern; the other noise which I associated with the Molly was the soughing noise of their wings as they came in to land immediately over one's head, hidden by the mist or low-lying cloud which was such a regular feature of the environment whenever one ventured on top of the island. So loud was the noise that one ducked instinctively every time it happened, even though the birds seemed to have some radar-like sense which enabled them to avoid obstacles, whether human or inanimate. On the rare days of clear visibility, it was a delight to watch them playing on the edge of the cliff, when they would swoop lazily towards the rising up-current, rise with it and then tumble sideways as it died out, then move back inland before repeating the process innumerable times.

There was one moment on that same day, with the whole Expedition scattered over the plateau of semi-impenetrable Tree fern, when an excited shout from Andrew, on a ridge leading towards the highest point, caused us all to look up. He had found a nestling Gony, a Wandering Albatross which we reckoned to be about nine months old and which seemed to weigh over twenty-five pounds. Its sheer size compared with the adult Mollys all around it brought home the bird-book distinction between 'very large' (Yellow-nosed) and 'outsize' (Wandering). The 'chick' put up with being picked up, measured and handled, with surprising placidity, not that it had much choice in the matter as it would be incapable of flight for at least another month [*See Plate 15*]. It regained its 'nest' with somewhat cumbrous dignity and settled down to await the return of one of its parents, an event which might not occur for another thirty-six hours.

I have already referred to several species by their Tristan names: the Gony, the Pieu (Pe-oo), the Molly and the Stinker; there were occasions when the Tristan name for a bird did lead to some confusion in nomenclature, particularly when Nelson referred to a Great Skua as a 'Shite-hawk,' whereas our Tristan 'vocab' had it clearly indicated as a Sea Hen. The ornithologist then made it worse by referring to something called a Bonxie, a term which we could only presume to be of Celtic origin but which we accepted as another example of clear scientific thinking ... The Great Shearwater, the bird on which both we and the Tristan Islanders subsisted for considerable periods, is called a 'Petrel' and various other members of the same family were designated as 'Haglet.' a term which I would associate much more readily with some of the female members of 2b than with the various ornithological varieties which came under that umbrella. The Soft-plumaged Petrel was called the 'Littlest White-breasted Haglet.' a designation which I could hardly risk applying to a female member of 2b without ending up in 'The News of the World,' just as the 'Black Haglet' appellation of the Great-winged Shearwater might have brought me up in front of the Race Relations Board. Tristan scientific terminology appeared to break down when it arrived at the Kerguelen Petrel, which was called a 'Blue Nighthawk,' though it must be recorded that the only two we captured during my stay were both caught at night; the 'Nightbird' name for the Prion seemed wholly illogical but why is the Antarctic Tern called a

'King-bird'? There seems to be some doubt as to whether the Penguin (Rockhopper) is a 'Pinnawin' or a 'Pinnamin' but one has only to observe the operations of the Common Diving Petrel at sea, minute though it is in comparison, to realise why it is called a 'Flying Pinnawin' (or 'Pinnamin') ...

The 3 November was such a fine calm day that seven members went up the mountain, five of them with the intention of staying at least one night on top and three of those five hoping to stay longer if weather conditions permitted. The two porters having descended, seven of us were resting after a very peaceful dinner that evening when there was a loud thump on the outside of the hut just above my ear (I was sitting on my bunk). I assumed that some people on top had decided to return early but when nobody came through the door, I went outside and immediately captured an unknown bird lying slightly dazed beneath the window. I think this was the first occasion that we caught a bird at night on the island and unfortunately Mike was one of the five on top, but we identified it as a White-faced Storm-petrel and released it after Ian had taken at least four photos[*See Plate 12*]. The next night was uneventful bird-wise, though the day was the one calm day when the barge could have come from Tristan had there not been a funeral there which coincided. It was a marvellous day for the surveyors, the ornithologist, the botanist and the Invertebrate Zoologist, who were all up on top, though the latter two walked in just as we were finishing dinner and as the wind was beginning to rise, the rain to fall ... After a terrible night on top, the remaining three walked in (much to my relief) at about 7.20 am on Guy Fawkes Day and spent most of the rest of it in their bunks, recovering, while the rest of us listened to the wind and the rain outside: my own escapist literature was John Buchan's 'The Island of Sheep'! There had been some suggestion of a bonfire (fuel?) and a barbeque, but the weather put paid to these ideas and it was with a sense of relief that in the thick mist conditions of the late evening we began to hear thumps against the walls of the hut, some actually against the window.

It was not just a good evening for the ornithologist: it was a good evening for almost everybody after the frustrations of the day. The ground outside the hut was alive with dazed birds, countless prions, dozens of Soft-plumaged Petrels and White-faced Storm-petrels, several White-bellied Storm-petrels, a couple of Little Shearwaters, a Kerguelen Petrel which was unfortunately slain in an effort to take a blood sample, and a couple of Common Diving Petrels. All these were caught with the aid of two or three rather feeble torches and were examined and weighed by our hard-pressed ornithologist, who nevertheless enjoyed the occasion very much: it was unfortunate that such weather conditions never prevailed again up to the end of November. My own excursion almost every (late) evening (with Mike) never produced much more than two or three birds which had been dazzled down by our weak lights.

The Bunting and Thrush watches were very much in the scientific order of things and one had to concentrate in a way which I found somewhat difficult (see Chapter 9) just as my views clashed with my scientific brethren on at least two occasions when I was desirous of getting my hands on dead shearwaters or their eggs for culinary purposes but was impeded by the meticulous, accurate measurement of each specimen, a process which took considerable time. When the odd rarity turned up, I was delighted to notice that my own materialistic approach which had been rejected by the others with some contempt, was mirrored in a conflict between the ornithologist and the Invertebrate Zoologist. On 1 November, when the surveyor and his mate correctly identified a strange 'wader' on the Skua bog, and the ornithologist and his mate not only identified but actually captured a White-rumped Sandpiper thousands of miles from home (see the Methuen Paperback edition of Bill Oddie's *Little Black Bird Book*, pages 55-56, and I hope he's suitably 'gripped off'), the attitude of the Invertebrate Zoologist was not only that it had to be thoroughly 'deloused' so that he could collect parasitic insects, but also that it should be killed and preserved for posterity, a sentiment which the ornithologist rejected most contumaciously and the bird was duly released. Luckily neither he nor the Invertebrate Zoologist ever got their hands on the three swallows which were also way off course at this time, but the Wilkin's Bunting which eventually strayed into the Rail trap made out of a crayfish pot on 8 November was a very different matter.

Personally I had been up the mountain doing a 'sched' with Gilfie, my usual companion, plus, on this occasion, Ian and Dick, so that none of us met the Tristan 'Big Canary' because we arrived back too late. It emerged that despite insistent demands from the Invertebrate Zoologist to 'kill it,' the ornithologist had only compromised so far as to permit a thorough 'delousing' before releasing the beautiful bird with the glowing amber plumage. I was sorry to have missed this event but the capture led to further investigation of Wilkin's Bunting habitat around the Skua Bog followed by further captures prior to my own assistance during the afternoon of 28 November, a day when we were all recovering from the effects of Andrew's birthday party. Joining the other ornithologists after lunch, I was privileged to watch the intrepid capture of a nesting Skua, unfortunately one which had already been ringed. A few moments later, a mist-net produced another cock Wilkin's which was duly examined, measured meticulously, 'deloused' and released, following the which procedure it wandered off on foot into the surrounding vegetation in a drunken fashion somewhat reminiscent of the events of the previous evening. Mike watched its progress sympathetically, muttered something like "Bugger that Richard's desire to catch bugs" (anyway there were a lot of bugs in it) and then turned to me and enquired if I realised that, apart from the likes of the California Condor, I had just been holding a specimen of one of the rarest birds in the world?

CHAPTER 9

REMEMBRANCE SUNDAY

"If we were on an isolated rock in a stormy sea," said Eugene, smoking with his eyes on the fire, "Lady Tippins couldn't put off to visit us, or, better still, might put off and get swamped. People couldn't ask one to wedding breakfasts. There would be no Precedents to hammer at, except the plain sailing Precedent of keeping the light up. It would be exciting to look out for wrecks."

"But otherwise," suggested Lightwood, "there might be a degree of sameness in the life."

"I have thought of that also," said Eugene, as if he really had been considering the subject in its various bearings with an eye to the business; "but it would be a defined and limited monotony. It would not extend beyond two people. Now, it's a question with me, Mortimer, whether a monotony defined with that precision and limited to that extent might not be more endurable than the unlimited monotony of one's fellow creatures."

Dickens: *Our Mutual Friend*

On Sunday, 21 November, I wrote in my diary 'You would think Sundays on Inaccessible were not as tedious as Sundays in the outside world but this is not the case - maybe it's because Nelson and Andrew won't fish on a Sunday ...'

The previous Sunday, 14 November, had been the first day when the mountain had been clear of cloud since the previous Wednesday and though we had found many useful things to do, the frustrations were beginning to mount up by the time that the 14th dawned bright and clear. In the twenty-four hours between the Thursday and Friday evenings, the Great Shearwaters had arrived from the other end of the Atlantic, tens of thousands of them, wheeling in the sky and adding a new unearthly cry to the night noises, something between an indignant baby's wail and a donkey's bray, staccato and diminuendo.

Porridge over, the surveyor and his assistant were the first to get away without, for once, the statutory fun about what they were having for lunch (could they be beginning to have confidence in the cook?) The botanist and the Invertebrate Zoologist's assistant hung around for half an hour while the Invertebrate Zoologist got himself ready and then they too set off in a vertical direction. Because of the fine weather, the others had all found things to do and had disappeared in different horizontal directions before I realised that there was no water in the containers and that the current paraffin drum was empty. By the time I had made good the deficiencies and had peeled and cooked the potatoes for the evening meal, it was time to start preparing lunch for the remaining seven.

I don't know whether it was the monotony of the lunch diet - the ritual beef tea and the venerable cheese accompanied by the electrician's bread, all parsimoniously divided into exactly equal shares, or whether it was the sight of Nelson composing himself for his two and a half-hour Sunday afternoon vigil solemnly gazing into the middle distance, or something in my face which made a deep impression on Andrew's consciousness. Whatever it was, at about quarter past one, as I was looking forlornly at the breakers roaring in from South America, Andrew appeared at my right shoulder.

"Jawn," he said, "you want to get some haigs?"

I had finished my last bottle of Bell's the week before and my immediate thought was that Andrew had some secret cache of which neither I nor any other Expedition member had cognisance, so I accepted with alacrity. Things became clearer as Andrew changed into his 'working' overalls, charged me to bring some plastic bags and observed over his shoulder that "dem bods is a-laying."

We set off, leaving Nelson righteously pious and the ornithologist organising bunting watches among the rather unenthusiastic non-ornithological remnant.

Following the now well-trodden path to the shore, we turned right along the shingle, Andrew in his moccasins and I in my climbing boots. We picked our way from stone to boulder, from boulder to pebble, from pebble to pebble, from pebble to pebble to stone to pebble to stone to boulder to stone to boulder to boulder to boulder with the roar of the surf blocking out all sound on our left and the precipices on our right becoming gradually more unscalable. Andrew moved lightly and efficiently, without apparent haste and not making it obvious that without me he could have reached his destination in about half the time that we were taking. Nevertheless even he only managed to avoid accidentally walking over a fur-seal by a matter of two stones, such was his concentration on his foot-placing, and we both watched, in my case luxuriating in the rest, as she made her way back to the sea, casting reproachful glances backwards from her liquid eyes.

I repressed the immortal words of Obelix:

"O les sales bêtes, et ça ne se mange même pas," knowing perfectly well that she could be eaten if only one were desperate enough. I recalled that Andrew was ten years older than I was and that I was supposedly a leader of the Expedition. We clambered round the promontory separating the first penguin rookery from the second and I gratefully followed Andrew's lead without getting wet. Communication was always difficult with Andrew because I couldn't understand what he said. With Nelson it was different because he couldn't hear what I said, but once I had made my message clear to Andrew, the latter could transmit it verbatim to Nelson who could then communicate perfectly clearly direct to me. On this occasion, there was no Nelson, still incommunicado in sphinx-like Sunday trance, so Andrew made contact by shout and gesture, combating both the roar of the surf and our mutual incomprehensibility by obvious goodwill.

We went from boulder to boulder, from boulder to stone to stone to stone to pebble to pebble to boulder to stone and the surf continued to pound on the shingle to our left. As Andrew drew ahead once again I was relieved to see him kick a profligate penguin to one side and draw up on the very edge where the shingle gave away to the six foot high tussock grass - a very definite edge and one which was clearly marked all the way round Blenden Hall though impossible to define once the cliffs became truly 'inaccessible.' Here, he took off his jersey and dropped it on the shingle about a yard from the tussock line. He looked at me, fully togged up for the Antarctic, smiled sympathetically and dived on all fours through a small hole in the tussock about two feet above his jersey. Tout à fait le 'White Rabbit.'

For a moment I remained horror-struck at his desertion, but a second later I plunged resolutely in his track (after all, if Alice could do it ...?)

The full odour did not hit me for at least a dozen yards as I was so preoccupied with catching up with my precursor whose presence became evident, after a certain amount of desperate scrabbling, by a view of the soles of his moccasins about ten yards along one of the numerous alleys offered to me - I had chosen the correct one because of the freshly turned earth in this particular channel. The soles kicked once, I gripped the earth and the odour rose up and hit me like a sledgehammer. Andrew was prostrate on his side, his right arm buried up to the shoulder in a hole in the ground. A further twitch and he retracted an indignant shearwater whose wingspan of at least four feet made one aware not only of his temerity but also of the extreme narrowness of the many scrapes into the multitudinous burrows.

"Petrel" was his dispassionate comment as he let the shearwater lumber myopically and harmlessly away. A yard to Andrew's right was another burrow. Full length on the damp and odorous earth, he plunged again, groped and muttered something about "bods" as the infantile donkey bray died away. He got back on all fours.

A yard further on and he plunged to his left but again his exploration of the burrow was unproductive and he moved upwards over a boulder and started to investigate a complex of at least five holes on his right. Determined to keep up, I rose to my feet, crouching, placed my right foot on the earth in front of the boulder and promptly descended two feet as the ground caved in. Indignant and hysterical cries arose. Andrew glanced backwards for a moment, grinned and continued to probe. A wriggle to the right and he disappeared between stalks of tussock.

Fronds whipping against my face I dived after him. Again I was faced by the soles of his moccasins. A moment later a hand came back towards me clutching a blotchy white egg about three times the volume of a hen's egg. I dug in my pocket and brought out a plastic bag in which I placed the treasure and thenceforth proceeded on all threes, my left hand being entirely occupied with protecting the 'bag.' Further delving into the five-hole complex proving unproductive, Andrew moved upwards again, this time to his left through another alleyway not immediately obvious to the uninitiated eye. Scraping, scratching, scrabbling and scrooging, I followed him, frequently on all threes, sometimes crouching, sometimes crawling on my stomach, left hand gallantly upholding the precious plastic bag in front of me.

We wandered up and we wandered down, we forked to the left and we corkscrewed right. Each time we paused there was the prospect of the soles of Andrew's feet as, flat on the evil-smelling soil, he prospected the infinite burrows, and once in a while, his hand would come back towards me clutching a large white egg, which I would carefully place in the plastic bag before plunging after him again through the uncharted tussock. For all I knew, we might have visited the same burrow eight times because they all looked identical, but Andrew never seemed to hesitate, even indulging in a U-turn which brought us out into head-high tussock where we could stand upright and see the clouds sailing above the island. The one constant factor was the roar of the surf and when I faced it, I knew that the island was behind me. The soft earth crumbled beneath me as I struggled to maintain contact and collect the rare offerings: on one occasion the hand produced a large indignant chick entirely covered with pale blue down almost the size of a shearwater but rotund. I glanced interrogatively and my guide proffered the answer. "Nightbird." Another example of the chick being infinitely larger than the adult bird - the Broad-billed Prion is about the same size as a turtle dove. The chick made no effort to re-enter its burrow when released but sat in its runway, powder blue, beautiful and fatly self-satisfied.

The ramifications of the rookery were infinite and I had nothing to do but follow the moccasins and collect the occasional egg, protecting the haul from breakage by upholding same as I progressed haphazardly through the dense tussock. After about an hour, Andrew parted some growth, considered for a moment and then swung sharply to his left before plunging his arm into the inevitable burrow. Seeing that he was unlikely to disappear for at least thirty seconds, I risked a glance in the area where he had looked and discovered that I was some seventy feet above the shingle with a sheer drop below my eyes and crumbling burrows beneath my knees. I backed away with some precipitation and discovered that I had lost Andrew. The only way that I could be sure of rejoining him was to regain the cliff-edge and follow in his tracks. Clutching the roots of the tussock, I edged my way after him and found him happily researching a complex of at least fifteen burrows some five yards from the edge of the cliff.

I decided that it was time I took a more active part in the proceedings, deposited my bag of eggs safely in a low-lying clump and ventured my gloved hand intrepidly into a surplus hole. Some ornithologist has described the Great Shearwater on Gough Island in the following terms: 'They have muscles like wildcats, claws like fishhooks and bills like daggers, and clearly represent one of nature's more spectacular success stories ...'

My experiment in egg collecting served to prove the validity of the ornithologist's thesis in that within five minutes I sustained a wound on my left forewrist of which I still bear the scar. My amateurish efforts did provoke an exodus from the burrows which showed how great was the underground population, not just of Great Shearwaters but of other varieties, particularly prions, showing that the laying and breeding pattern on Inaccessible was not exactly co-ordinated. By the time I had investigated one burrow, Andrew had disappeared in a south-westerly direction and despite my proximity to the cliff, I felt it better to stay more closely to my guide, particularly as my own researches had produced no eggs for the bag. The act of placing one's hand down the burrow and groping around the 'nest' of a laying shearwater, oneself totally blind and the shearwater ditto but disadvantaged by the fact that she is totally unused to the human presence, is not exactly a sensual experience though I suppose it must have been the nearest one could get to one on Inaccessible. At the request of the other members of the Expedition I will therefore refrain from further description, as the ribaldry to which it gave rise in the hut showed that this matter does not lie in the line of pure scientific research.

Andrew was doing something which he and his forebears had been doing for generations, just as they had been hunting the 'Mollys' for Sunday roasts and knocking off the Skuas and the penguin for bait since the time of Corporal Glass. I didn't know how many thousands or even millions of shearwater had arrived on Inaccessible to breed but I did know that however many eggs Andrew and I took, it would make only an infinitesimal difference to the total world population of 'Puffin Majeur.' The eggs themselves, though they could be described generically as large, white and oval, were of infinite variety within the bounds of that general description. They were so large that the female Great Shearwater laid only one egg and if that were broken or taken, apparently she was unable to re-lay. Insofar as their culinary destination was concerned, all that mattered was that they should be gathered within twenty-four hours of their being laid but once gathered, they would keep for at least a fortnight without artificial means of preservation. (Dixerat Nelson.)

However fine the weather, the 'Petrels' had only just arrived and Andrew and I were pushing our luck by egg-hunting so early. For two hours Andrew pushed his luck into over two hundred burrows and our total bag at the end was seventeen 'haigs.' I ought to say total 'bags' because by the time we had ten, I had started another on the well-known principle of not putting all your 'haigs' ... I ought also to say that by the time we had gathered seventeen 'haigs,' I was not only totally exhausted, but also completely and abysmally disoriented. During our wanderings it had occurred to me that it was miraculous that the shearwaters should be capable not only of navigating ten thousand miles to the two tiny islands of Nightingale and Inaccessible but that once there, they could then find their way to their own individual burrow among so many apparently identical thousands. What was even more miraculous was the ability of my guide to lead me, clutching my two plastic bags, down a tunnel which emerged on to shingle where the surf continued to pound and where, about a yard away from our exit point, lay his discarded jersey ...

Once there I issued iron rations of Kendal Mint Cake thereby restoring my authority as quartermaster at least in my own mind if not in Andrew's (where it was unlikely that the matter had ever arisen). We retraced our route most delicately, the more so that I had ditched one of the plastic bags on Andrew, and the portage thereof restricted even his mobility. Twice I slipped, the second time actually falling full length, but still upholding the booty in my left hand above the shingle, much to the relief of my guide who gave me another approving grin. When we reached the hut, it was empty apart from Nelson who was still in somnambulistic trance. There was a note from the ornithologist - 'If you want to do a bunting watch, try number 4.' A note was as good as a wink and having made arrangements for the refreshment of returning explorers, I sallied forth again into the late afternoon sunshine complete with pencil and notebook. Buntings number 4 had chosen a site in the tussock above our original tent site just off the track which led up the mountain. There was a convenient stone as a seat which commanded almost a panoramic view of the sea directly in front of Blenden Hall and once one had noted the first sign of activity on the part of the nesting birds, one had ten minute intervals of contemplation during which the mind could wander, lulled by the wavesong, the passing clouds and the still warm sunshine.

After about four minutes there was a loud twitter and the cockbird arrived from my right rear, sat on the spray directly over the nest, twittered some more and the hen emerged from below. She sat beside him and he fed her something with which she disappeared. A moment later she re-emerged, nagged him sharply for a moment and then flew off with him in the direction of Tristan da Cunha on my right. Having made suitable entries in my notebook, I waited some six minutes before she reappeared with only a minimal chirrup and dived swiftly out of sight into the nest. I knew then there was likely to be a ten minute interval before the return of the cock and let my mind wander with the Yellow-nosed Albatross which chose this moment to float across high above me.

Try as I could the full version of Baudelaire's poem would not come to mind, though I could reproduce at least three-quarters. The lines which particularly echoed on this occasion were:

Le poète est semblable au prince des nuées, and the final:
Ses ailes de géant l'empêchent de marcher.

Knowing how little impression I could make with such references among the arid scientific wastes wherein I dwelt, I meditated on an exchange overheard the previous day between two of the young men who were disputing about how to make the wind generator work more efficiently.

"You are," said a voice, crushingly, "about as scientific as John Woolley!"

Despite the fact that I was swelling with pride, his interlocutor had been at a loss for words.

I became aware that a Starchy was pecking inquisitively at my left boot and side-footed it skilfully into the undergrowth. The noise produced an excited Rail 'cheep cheep' and an adult whizzed across the track immediately to my right. My energetic lunge missed by about a yard and a half and I looked around guiltily to make sure that no other member of the Expedition was within viewing distance, though there was no reason why any should have been. Recomposing myself I became aware of more Rail noises and was just settling into the requisite immobility when another loud twitter announced the return of the bunting cock.

Dutifully I noted movements but my notes failed to record the febrile excitement of the two buntings - the hen would become so impatient that if the cock did not appear within two minutes of what she considered to be the appointed time, she would swoop off the nest with a tremendous clatter, judging to perfection his late arrival even without the warning twitter. (So that the poor old lad was invariably caught with the half-empty pint in his hand about twenty yards short of the nest.) As I was there in the interests of pure scientific research there was little I could do in the interests of male chauvinism except observe helplessly and record intelligently as the cock was pecked into submission.

The Rails continued to cheep in the ten-minute intervals and, unable as I was to catch one, I was often rewarded with the same thrill which I have already recorded - the 'cheep cheep' repeated a hundred times and then suddenly the little purple/ brown/ black visitor, head to one side, red eye agog but usually completely oblivious of the human presence eighteen inches to his or her left!

The ocean stretched vastly before me and the buntings came and went and the breakers continued to break. Evening noises began to impinge and a cloud of shearwaters began to wheel over the sea and the cliffs. Apart from their movements and noises, I watched the Brown Noddies returning to their nests in the Phylica trees two hundred metres behind me. The banshee wail of the Sooty Albatross three hundred metres higher indicated some movement which I could not detect even with the field-glasses and the truncated curlew noise of the Softies in the tussock below me indicated the apparent return of some more conscript ornithologists.

Having become accustomed to the shearwater baby bray, I was unprepared for a new cacophony which was suddenly added to the evening hymn. My initial impression was that it was some benighted woman wailing for her demon lover. My acute awareness of the entire absence of women on Inaccessible immediately contradicted this view and anyway, though we could well muster one or two lovers from our ragged ranks, none of the few could exactly qualify in the 'demon' category. I listened more attentively and realised that it was only the surveyor yodelling to his mate as he came down the mountains. The cock bunting having made its most recent visit, and I having been there for an hour and a quarter, I went back to the hut to cook dinner.

Rashly, perhaps, I decided to make a potato omelette, using one shearwater egg per client. I chopped up my potatoes and

mingled with them powdered garlic, dehydrated mushroom soup
and mixed herbs in very limited quantities. The trouble about an
omelette, even with shearwater eggs, was that one felt it wouldn't
fill the basic trough in the stomach of the young, but Ian had made
a good stodgy cake the day before and I hoped that some Instant
Whip added to the cake would fill the gaps. Cooking semi-happily
away I listened to the chat of the returned heroes -

"I'm sure it was a Wilkin's."

"Nelson, you should have seen the driftwood beyond the
Skua bog."

"What's for supper?"

"I don't know what you've been doing, Andrew, but you look
a bit shattered."

Voice of the ornithologist:

"There are two notebooks missing."

"What's for supper?"

"Andrew, where did you go?"

Nick appeared in the kitchen, he and his retinue having
arrived some half an hour earlier.

"OK?"

"Yep. You too?"

I pushed my apéritif bottle at him and he took the habitual
swallow - I followed his example.

"Good day?"

"Yes. We got plenty of specimens even though I know a lot
are duplicates. What did you do?"

I told him and told him what was for supper and, before he
could ask, how much there would be per person.

"Have I got time to go for a wash?"

"Sure - at least three quarters of an hour."

He went, thoughtfully carrying an empty water container to
refill. The ornithologist entered quietly.

"Any drinks going, John?"

"What do you want, Mike? Orange, coffee or alcohol?"

"Just orange, John. The lads are a bit parched."

"Good day?"

"Very good."

If Mike was pleased, there was reason for hope, but my rising optimism was quelled by the ensuing inevitable enquiry.

"Are you doing fish-cakes for dinner?"

(Why the hell did I do an entrée last night just because I'd got six unexpected eggs?)

"Sorry, Mike, omelette tonight."

"That'll be a nice change, John."

I kept the rings going and fiddled with the controls on the cooker, more or less as a propitiatory gesture to the Gods of Chance. The surveyor came in through the kitchen door and I pushed a long, soft drink at him. It emerged that he had had a good day too, but where was his mate? The mate had gone in through the front door and I went in to find him loudly enquiring how the skivers had been getting on. Luckily, a tolerant voice squashed him before I could give tongue.

I served supper and was pleased to observe that though the culinary heights of the previous evening were not achieved, the 'omelette' (for want of a better word) was still appreciated.

Some two hours later, after the ritual game of whist which was duly won by Nelson and Andrew, it was birdcatching time. On this particular evening, there seemed to be very few which could be distracted by torchlight and despite the sodden nature of the undergrowth, my cynegetic instincts led me further afield than usual even though I had neglected to don waterproof trousers. A new shearwater colony was beginning to proliferate on the banks of the rivulet behind the hut and I decided to utilise my freshly acquired skills as a burrow-groper. The immediate results were the capture of an indignant bird with which I stumbled back to the darkened hut where I was pleased to see light at the scientist's end. Mike was ringing another shearwater with the assistance of Nick and David. I pushed my bird at David and went out again.

By this time my trousers were sopping but I went straight back to the colony site. 'Straight,' of course, is a relative term on Inaccessible terrain at night, but some time later I extracted another shearwater with the casual insouciance of someone who had performed the feat successfully at least twice before and was promptly pecked down the side of my left nostril. Blood up, both metaphorically and physically, I carried him back to the hut.

They looked at me.

"Bloody hell" said Mike.

I gave him the shearwater and went to bed. Altogether a very satisfactory day.

Ornithologist with Wandering Albatross chick

CHAPTER 10

SONG OF MYSELF

J'ai eu pitié des autres
probablement pas assez,
and at moments that suited my own convenience
Le paradis n'est pas artificiel,
l'enfer non plus.
Ezra Pound: [Pisan] *Cantos LXXVI*

For months after I returned from the South Atlantic, I kept meeting people who knew where I had been and who invariably asked me, "Did you enjoy yourself?" Supposing that they wanted an accurate answer, which was probably a fallacious supposition in at least eighty per cent of the enquiries, I would explain that 'enjoy' was the wrong word: there had been several moments when I had longed to be safely home, even teaching 5b, but that I wouldn't have missed the experience for the world. Following one of the worst nights of storm, when sheets of felt were ripped off the roof and the wind generator was broken, apparently beyond repair, I decided to read *King Lear* during the afternoon because, to quote my diary, 'it rather matched my mood.' The diary entry for that day concludes 'In the first act of *Lear*, Regan says about her father 'yet he hath ever but slenderly known himself.' If and when I get off this island, I hope I shall know myself better.'

If there were several moments on the island when I felt depressed, there was none perhaps more poignant than the evening of 3 November when Dick returned with Nelson from the mountain (where they had left five others to spend a couple of nights) bringing news from the 'sched' that there were now no places available on *Tristania II* in December and that the Royal Navy would not be arriving until February. This news was a source of delight to all the young men and I could share their pleasure - after all, they had been led to expect that the Expedition would last at least four months, even if the rations were calculated to last for at least a hundred days ... Most of them appreciated my personal dismay and sympathised not only with my position as a headmaster with a limited leave of absence, but also as a 'père de famille toujours responsable.' Whenever such moments of depression overtook me, my mind would wander, despite the warning deeply etched in it (and recorded somewhere in my diary):

.... *Nessun maggior dolore*
Che ricordarsi del tempo felice
Nella miseria .....

The 3 November coincided exactly with the half-term period six years previously when Sylvie and I had spent four days walking through the moors and dales some ten miles inland from the coast where we lived. That night I reviewed those walks in minute detail as I lay, quite unable to sleep, hour after uncomfortable hour.

We had stayed in the Goathland Hotel, renowned throughout the area for its comfort and cuisine. Thence, the first morning, we had sallied forth along a disused railway track heading south, until we came to the moors. We plunged into the heather, trying to chart our course via the burnt patches in the absence of an identifiable route and arguing cheerfully about the right direction until, miles further on, we crossed the beaten motor way of the Lyke Wake Walk at right angles and were able to take a reverse bearing. I had caught up with Madame's initial burst, so we had time to appreciate the rocketing forth of the grouse at unexpected moments likely to bring pleasure to the game-keeper's heart - the appearance of the odd out-of-season curlew did nothing to add to my vain struggle to make it clear to her ladyship's mind that a curlew is a curlew is a curlew, whereas a peewit is a lapwing is a green plover or any other silly name.

Miles further on still, we found a stile and a clear path through some meadows and woods, eventually straying into a conifer plantation which descended steeply into the river valley of Newton Dale on our left. The path soon petered out and the undergrowth was thick with brambles whose wet fruit was still palatable despite Madame's certainty that by now 'le Diable aurait pissé là-dessus.' After about half an hour of struggling descent we emerged on to a forestry track which in turn led us to the bottom of a foot-path which, in its turn, reclimbed the side of the valley which we had just come down. By the time we had finished arguing about who had misread the map and had made our way up to Newton-on-Rawcliffe, it was half-past one but the *White Swan* was open, even if we were the only customers. Apart from the wetness of the undergrowth during our scramble down the valley, a thin drizzle had been seeping through us during the last mile and we sat before a splendid fire, sipping a delicious home-made soup accompanied by appropriate quantities of Real Ale. As we moved on to sandwiches stuffed with beef, turkey, ham, cheese and salad, we began to gossip and catch up with local news - a subject on which Sylvie was much more expert than myself (I am known in the *White Swan* as 'Sylvie's husband')...

It required a positive effort to take leave of the warmth, both of our welcome and the atmosphere, but we knew that our route back was longer than the morning's eleven odd miles, though there was no danger of our straying on the return journey. The lane switch-backed between the farmlands, usually in a straight line, and as there was no traffic we could argue happily and uninterruptedly about the probable line of the Roman Road. We traversed the straggling village of Stape, lost in the midst of the moors, boasting, as far as I could see, four chapels and no pub and therefore, deservedly lost. Beyond the last house the road dipped into a valley and, when it began to climb up to the moors again on the far side, became a rough chalk and flint surface. Thin drizzle drifted across from the heather on our left and when the conifer plantation to our right finally came to an end, we saw the exposed surface of the Roman Road marching straight as a die through the valleys, diagonally across our own route. There was a gate to open ...and, as I thought about it, another memory of that gate interrupted the previous flow of recollection ...to a more recent occasion, about two years earlier when Mike and Elizabeth Swales had been staying with us: we had gone out in the car for a picnic lunch near Hutton-le-Hole. Returning via the Roman road route, we had arrived at this same gate with another car just behind us and in politely holding it for the strangers to pass, we had allowed three moorland sheep to slip through which set off at a smart trot in a southerly direction. The strange car produced a middle-aged man and a teenaged youth with whom Michael, I and my youngest set off, in pursuit of the erring flock, leaving Sylvie with instructions to be ready to open and shut the gate quickly if and when we succeeded in herding them back. It wasn't an easy task to overtake the sheep and start them moving in the right direction but the middle-aged stranger, whose face seemed familiar, showed quiet determination as did Mike and after about quarter of an hour's plunging through damp heather, the sheep were once more safely grazing in their lawful abode. We bade farewell to the strangers and drove on across the moor.

"I'm sure I know that man's face," I observed.

"Not surprising," said Michael. "That was David Sheppard, the Bishop of Liverpool."

Appropriate, really.

Again, I started reliving the walks with Sylvie, but having thought about Mike, my mind now switched from landscape to landscape, event to event, and even meal to meal. One of the penalties of having a good memory is the pain of total recall in adverse circumstances, so that by 7 November I was writing in my diary:

'When I get back to Yorkshire, I am going to make a tour of all the places like Beckhole, Runswick Bay and Ravenscar - with Sylvie and the family, whether they like it or not - just like brother Andrew used to do and still does sometimes - I know much better why he does it: Inaccessible is often as big a bore as his job.'

By the 19th, the situation had deteriorated insofar as my communings with the diary were concerned.

'Fog and mist - no sign of the three on the mountain at 9 am but this is not surprising as they are camping in the Phylica on the far side.

'Another thoroughly miserable day - it will be a good thing

for me when (and if!) this barge or launch does come - I have been
on the island too long and now I do not have enough to do - there
are moments when there is far too much for one pair of hands but
there are also some periods as long as two hours with nothing
except Dickens or Shakespeare (both of whom have had a fairly
good going over). Images of places where I have been happy keep
springing up in my mind - Runswick Bay with Sylvie, Newcastle
with Simon, the forests around Vichy with Nicky (my no. 2),
Somerset with Alison and the Churnet Valley with PB (the
youngest). They are persistent and occur unexpectedly at any
time of day - I find I can hardly bear to look at the photos at the
back of this diary.'

Dickens and Shakespeare had indeed had a good going over.
Diary entry for 26 October:
'The batteries on my cassette recorder don't seem to last very
long and I am being miserly with the amount of music I play (much
to the relief of the others!) Of course another reason that I feel
isolated is that I am the only non-scientist - thank God for Dickens
and Stendahl!'
What my diary doesn't record is the sheer discomfort of the
hut when one was trying to read. Though I was privileged in that
not only did I have one of the two single bunks, I had the one under
the only window. This meant that during daylight hours everybody
used it: the postmaster and his assistant used it for stamping and
franking their envelopes, the botanist used it for arranging his
plants in their presses, the ornithologist used it for disembowelling
and dissecting dead birds, the Invertebrate Zoologist (despite his
monopoly of the space in the scientist's room) used it for counting
and preserving insects, everybody used it for sitting on to eat
meals or for simply sitting on and when a Starchy paid us a social
visit, it was too easy to guess whose bunk he would choose for
perching on ... Having been practically blind in my left eye since
my early teens (my optician was astonished to discover that my
general vision had actually improved after the Expedition), I
could only read in the hut if I could establish a position near the

top end of my bunk, my back against the wall but the light coming through the window over my left shoulder. Here I did not impinge on the activities of the others using the bunk as a table and facing the window. My own visibility once assured, I could usually manage to read for about an hour by dint of putting my sleeping-bag between my back and the wall and sometimes finding a box on which to rest my feet: concentration became difficult after about seventy-five minutes because I became too aware of physical malaise, whether it were pain in the shoulder from some projection in the wall, or pins and needles in a foot because it had been hanging too long in space. I remember reflecting that whereas I had always dreamed of being put in the 'Desert Island' situation and requesting Plomley to supply my wife as my one luxury, I would probably now choose to indulge in the glorious redundancies of an armchair.

Two of the young men had brought cassette recorders of a much more recent vintage than my own and these were equipped with ear-phones, so there was always a certain amount of competition to borrow them in the evening. Knowing that most of the young men disliked my music as much as I disliked theirs, I took advantage of my turn when the owners were feeling generous and could thereby enjoy a much more impressive quality of sound than anything my steam-driven machine could produce, without having to inflict anything on the others. On one such occasion, having listened to the first two movements of Beethoven's Fifth Piano Concerto (which I probably hadn't listened to for the previous five years) with great enjoyment, I dozed happily off to sleep despite the discomfort of the sitting position on my bunk and awoke some forty minutes later to find that I had been treated to a Rock concert on a cassette which had been surreptitiously substituted for the Beethoven. The young men were delighted. As I had slept through it, so was I.

I think that it was with Dick that I had a discussion about 'Desert Island' music. At that time (18 November?) apart from a Beethoven Piano Sonata which I had heard Simon practising over a period of six months and which I still loved, plus Buxtehude's

"Alles, was ihr tut" was firm for Handel (*Silent Worship* and a duet from the middle of 'Xerxes') and all the rest of J S Bach. It is no doubt typical of all people who are actually permitted to take part in the Plomley programme that they acknowledge that their tastes change and they say, much later, that they would now choose differently. Discussing it with Sylvie about fifteen months later, I discovered that I couldn't do without the second movement of Ravel's Piano Concerto in G, nor without the basic theme of 'Boris Godunov.'

"Why do you like Mussorgsky?" she enquired.

"Probably because he died of drink at the age of forty-two." I told her.

She fell silent.

Perhaps uninhabited islands increase the astringency of one's tastes.

Taste and variety were the two governing factors in my preparation of the main meal of the day, even though it was almost always a success because of the sheer hunger of the clientèle.

I enjoyed the evenings: they gave me an opportunity to listen, so that I knew what people were feeling and, very occasionally when I knew what was wrong, the chance to chat quietly to somebody, usually arising out of the taste of the meal or the horrors of washing-up. They also gave me a chance to read, or to listen to music, if the light was not too far away or if it was my turn with the earphone cassette recorder. Most of all the evenings gave me a chance to indulge in my cynegetic instincts and also a chance to feel that I was contributing something apart from meals. Even when I was not deliberately bird-watching, I seemed to be lucky. On 7 November, leaving the area of the hut to answer the call of nature and picking my way through the tussock, my feeble torch-ray picked out a large browny-grey bird upon which I jumped expeditiously, and which turned out to be a Kerguelen Petrel. As the only previous capture of this species had been sacrificed two days earlier on the altar of pure scientific research, Mike was very pleased, but I got an equal pleasure almost every evening when I would set out between half-past nine or ten, usually accompanied by Mike or David, sometimes by myself, sometimes with a lantern but usually only with a torch.

It was astonishing how the terrain differed within only two hundred yards of the hut, even though the differences were exaggerated by the darkness. The best catching-nights were those of mist and fog and light rain, but even on clear nights and even with only the weak torch, I would lie in the reasonably thin, dry tussock to the south, watching the enormous to and fro traffic above my head between land and sea, listening to the weird variety of cries and calls 'piercing the night's dull ear' above the surf-roar and, when all sounds failed, quite happy with the wheel of the unfamiliar stars.

Behind the hut, to the east, there was quite a deep marshy valley with thick tussock on its slopes. Such was the profusion of shearwaters that they had started a new colony here and I made several nocturnal excursions to pull them out of their burrows to be ringed. Locating the exact area which was emitting the cacophonic bray was quite difficult because one never knew if one's next step was not going to involve one in a five-foot drop, followed by the immersion of one's boots in either water or mud. On one occasion, having crawled some twenty-five yards in order to extract a squawking bird, I had to spend some five minutes orienteering before I could decide in which direction lay the hut: the release of that particular shearwater was only approximately close to its capture point ...

One great source of pleasure was my increasing fitness. I never suffered from the hunger which certainly afflicted the young men and I could usually afford to pass on my own share of cakes, biscuits and sweets; nevertheless I was losing weight steadily (probably because of the 'no alcohol till evening' regime as much as anything). Certainly my activities on 27 November compared with what I did on 27 October show a change which had come about so gradually that I had hardly been aware of it. I had spent the morning of 27 November preparing huge quantities of food for Andrew's birthday and after lunch, the ornithologist invited me to join a shearwater-ringing party, an invitation which I was incautious enough to accept. We crossed the valley behind the hut, ignoring the burrows in that area, and began to climb the steep, thickly-tussocked cliff. Hard work though it was, it was a good job that the tussock was thick because the cliff soon became precipitous and it was difficult to keep up with Nelson and Andrew. We had been climbing and ringing for about an hour and a half and were still moving away from the hut when I realised that I would have to leave my companions and return if I were to be on the upper plateau in time for the 'sched' at 4.15. The sensible way to descend would have been to get on top of the tussock and roll down but my frequent efforts to attempt this feat were thwarted by the weakness of the individual tussock stalks, so my sub-tussock progress was charted with amusement by my fellow-ringers above, particularly when I arrived at the marshy bit at the bottom: they were shouting directions which of course I couldn't hear because I was too close to the shore. Having done a complete change of clothing, I started the ascent of West Road, the route to the upper plateau which lay on the other side of the valley. That was the day when I had agreed to pace Ian and in the process achieved my own record time, which was received with such respect by Nick and Dick, who met us at the 'sched' rendez-vous, that my self-esteem was greatly enhanced.

The boys were touchingly concerned about my decrepitude and saluted my odd achievement most flatteringly. By and large, they were incredibly competent and were capable of doing a variety of things without being asked, particularly when they were working together as a team. Not only could they cope, they could adapt to changing circumstances and they could fend for themselves when they had to; witness their ability to slow down when they realised I couldn't keep up!

If in my opinion I don't rate my leadership on Inaccessible very highly, it is because I didn't manage to make enough contact with the young men entrusted to my charge. I tried hard but there were two barriers to break through apart from the inevitable 'schoolmaster' label: the first was age which in the end was probably not so important because the second, the 'clan' syndrome, had already done its work. Their own versions of what they had done at 'Coll' were still the only experiences they had had which they deemed worthy of recollection (recollection of childhood experiences at that age are distinctly non-rigueur) and they were quite happy to go on repeating their experiences to each other. The only contacts with reality that they had yet made had been made largely in the same environment, so they were inclined to cling together when performing the countless essential useful tasks that they performed. Relatively spacious though the kitchen was, the cooker was so tiny that there was hardly room for more than one person to operate around it: nevertheless I had to struggle for about a month to make the point that ONE assistant per day was quite sufficient - it took that time to give them enough self-confidence to operate even in pairs rather than trios, apart from Dick, who knew exactly what he was doing, and Ian who amiably thought he did.

Their contact with each other and their ability to tolerate each other's previously known weaknesses served in my mind only to heighten my personal sense of being intolerant. My diary records several self-reproaches about my inadequacy but as my diary was the only companion to which I could always complain (my most precious possession), it is hardly surprising that the loneliness theme recurs far more often therein.

I would listen to their endless soliloquies about how they had dealt with the idiosyncrasies of various members of staff at 'Coll,' the staff-members being designated by patronymics which I could not recognise. If I intervened when I eventually heard an ancient name, even though they listened (or courteously appeared to), I felt that my observations were those of some antediluvian predecessor which could have little relevance to those of the needs of the imperious young. It would be unfair were I not to point out at this stage that the aforesaid young were frequently jarred by my imperious manner.

Possibly the only occasion when they took me seriously was when I was lecturing them on the care of the frying-pan, at a time so early after the building of the hut that I had still not yet made my unilateral decision to be responsible myself for all major washing-up.

"This, gentlemen, is a frying-pan. After use, it requires cleaning ONLY with a soft cloth and hot water. It should then be given a light (very light) covering of oil from the tin to the left of the cooker. If anybody touches it with a pan-scourer, or forgets to put on the oil, I will personally kick him in the balls ..."

Dead silence.

Message received and understood.

Quite often, on the other hand, I was running round like the fly with the ultra-marine fundament, simply in order to record people's opinions and pick their brains.

My diary for 30 October runs as follows, in its entirety:

'Cornflakes for breakfast, bread for lunch already made yesterday and no potatoes to cook and peel because it's macaroni tonight - an easy day!

'How Alison would laugh if she could see me eating cornflakes for breakfast, drinking water and chewing gum and Kendal Mint Cake! The water has had no ill-effects and I have not come out in heat lumps so far - I think I feel fitter but I must admit that I am looking forward to a tot by about 5.30 pm.

'I went right on the second penguin rookery to the north - they are much more numerous and tamer. Andrew and Nelson were fishing in that area and I came back carrying about eight large Five Fingers in each hand - a long tiring walk on the shingle.'

(Interjection eighteen months later: 'The thin string going through the gills and out through the mouths tying the fish together was cutting into my hands so much that by about the half-way stage, I stopped, cut chunks out of some convenient flotsam rope, connected the string to the rope, which was much more comfortable in my hand and so proceeded happily to the hut, where my arrival complete with burdens was saluted respectfully ... later even by Andrew and Nelson.')

Diary continues:

'In the end they (Nelson and Andrew) must have caught fifty-plus by quarter-past one and I had a hell of a job deciding what to do with them. In the end I salted a bucket-load of big fillets, set aside a fry for Monday and cooked a whole saucepan full for fish pie tomorrow night. Supper was Nelson's fish from yesterday, fried!

'The wind and swell grew worse in the afternoon and Clive and Joe came down early. I tried soaking porridge in brandy to catch Rails, but so far it hasn't worked.'

It was the bucket-load of fillets which was beginning to attract my attention by 6 November. Desperate though I was not to lose this extra source of protein (and variety!) the bucket undoubtedly 'ponged' and even though Nelson was in favour of eating the contents, when I consulted the others he was in a minority of one, Nick and the other senior members having decided views on the dangers of botulism. Consigning the fillets back to the sea was one of the bitterest of my experiences, and 6 November was a very black day.

There were many good days, for example, 1 November, the day of the White-rumped Sandpiper.

Clive and Joe, starting their survey of the Skua Bog area, had intelligently realised that what they had seen was not a regular South Atlantic species, so they had shuttled back to the hut to report. From their description (I record this fact with due modesty), my own immediate comment was 'Sandpiper' whereas the ornithologist was heard to mutter something about 'Stints.' I managed an hour off in the morning to go and look but saw nothing whatsoever and got very wet. After lunch, the weather was so awful that nearly everybody stayed indoors but the intrepid ornithologist, accompanied by his assistant, went back to the Skua Bog and identified a White-rumped Sandpiper. I have recorded its capture in Chapter 8, but have failed to convey the sense of achievement which we all felt that evening. Proper explorers would have been less fussy about meal-times than I was (but proper explorers in our circumstances would certainly have had more facilities for keeping things hot) - nevertheless when Mike and David came back very late after releasing their capture, I had managed to keep something reasonably warm for them and the ensuing celebrations were most enjoyable - my own mixture of different offerings allowed me to sleep uninterruptedly from 10 pm till 6 am, which was certainly the only occasion when I achieved such a lengthy period of continuous repose on Inaccessible Island.

Woolley may have been unhappy at various moments but by and large he was not moaning, not even to his diary. Maybe this was because there was sometimes a ship, an unexpected but welcome ship, in our parish; this compensated to some extent for the lack of visits from the Tristan barge/longboats which we had been led to believe would occur on the average once every ten days. In fact, as recorded elsewhere, the first time we had any physical contact with people from outside our world following our landing was six weeks later, when the barge and the new launch arrived for a re-embarkation which may have been well-timed for the convenience of our hosts on Tristan but, by 29 November, we had suffered a certain amount of psychological wear and tear.

Thus, when the *Hilary* hove into view on 27 October, her siren blaring to indicate that she wanted to talk to us, our vain efforts to make contact via Albert's useless radio were rendered less frustrating by the fact that here was a ship, only half a mile away. Our walkie-talkie on the top plateau had made contact and, even though *Hilary*'s Captain's response to all our requests was invariably "Negative, negative, negative," (- I learnt to know him later as 'Big Fat Dickie' but to the others he was 'Negative, negative, negative' for ever) nevertheless, here was a ship, presumably with lifeboats, which had clearly been asked to show some interest in our welfare. The *Hilary* presence was intermittent for the next couple of weeks but we were all galvanised into life on 31 October - I quote my diary for the whole day:

'The patent Woolley Rail trap hadn't worked this morning either - I have just been to look while the water was boiling for tea. A grey windy morning but there is a hint of blue in the sky. Wind generator propeller going like mad.

'Just as I finished the washing-up at 8.05 am, *Agulhas* came into view round North Point - wild excitement. She apparently had all our extra stores on board so she must have arrived early at Tristan, but the sea was too rough and she sailed past round to the south, Captain Leith saying over the radio that he was going back to Tristan. There was no further sighting during the day.

'I went to watch Rails during the afternoon but all I found was a variety of Nightshade which seemed to give Nick some pleasure. Some signs of discontent today: Mike felt that the young were not watching birds consistently enough, Richard wanted more help with bugs and geology and Joe wanted more bread baked every day (I told him he could do it himself). Then Dick put a note in the Log to say that he was unhappy (a) about hygiene standards and (b) about personal remarks. Could be a timely warning at this stage.

'On page 388 of *Bleak House* I found: 'I had never known before how short life really was, and into how small a space the mind could put it.'

'Listened to the *Emperor* on David's head-phones - a very different affair from my miserable cassette-recorder.

'Alison must have gone back after half-term.'

The doings of my favourite daughter were one of the themes which would run through my mind while doing a bunting watch somewhere to the south-east of the hut on a lovely day like 23 November, when I was bronzing happily in the sunshine. My diary says 'Mozart Piano Sonata K545.' How I came to be musing on such esoteric matters, conscious of the warmth of the sun and the fairly regular comings and goings of the buntings (which I was faithfully recording), I'm not sure. I was aware that I was in danger of getting burnt but was feeling contented because I had been to look at Wilkins Buntings with Mike, had collected Skua pellets and had enjoyed a long interesting conversation. Nelson and Andrew had come back with thirty-eight shearwaters and had promised to fish in the afternoon. God was in his Heaven and all was right with the world ...

Then, suddenly, there was this enormous blast on a siren - my diary continues:

'A ship! Bearing down on Blenden Hall from the south-west. Everybody converged on the hut - by the time I got there, Gilfie was already calling on the walkie-talkie ('Denstone Expedition to unknown ship, Denstone Expedition to unknown ship; come in please'). It turned out to be *Tristania II* of course and a moment later Captain Warren was asking for John Woolley and did he have any news for Peter Walker? He is going to be fishing around here from now until about December 5th but there is no question of his getting us off - this is still up to the Islanders. A very cheering conversation - he had obviously had several 'scheds' with Peter because he seemed to know all about Sylvia (who, he said, was well, as was the rest of the family) and to whom he promised to pass on love when he next spoke to North Yorkshire.'

We had some riotous moments during a conversation a couple of days later when my too punctilious 'Captain' caused Peter Warren to request that I should call him 'Peter' as he couldn't get used to being called 'Captain' on the radio. Having just learnt the correct way of expressing agreement over the ham radio, my answer of "OK, Roger, over" produced an indignant "Not Roger, Peter!" by which time the ornithologist and his mate (who had already evolved a private method of communication in ham radio South Africanese) were rolling about the floor in helpless mirth. The confusion became even worse following my return home when I took my twelve-year old Peter with me to Peter Walker's house on an evening when he had a 'sched' with Peter Warren somewhere in the middle of the South Atlantic ...

It is no accident that there are several accounts of agreeable conversations in this chapter, nor that they usually occurred in 'one to one' situations: I don't know how much I helped other members of the Expedition but I know how much some of them helped me, perhaps (though this is not recorded in Chapter 6) Gilfie as much as anybody because he was so frequently my companion; after the first month he was prepared to talk to me about his feelings on almost any topic, nor did he seem to suffer from having to listen to me in turn.

Of course, everybody helped practically. There was a continuous need for supplies of fresh water and anybody going towards the washing area without an extra burden was expected to take an empty plastic nasty for refilling. Similarly, as the refuse built up in the black plastic nasty by the kitchen door, people would volunteer to take it away and burn it: the disposal was usually efficient because we realised that tins would eventually rust away if thrown far enough into the sea following incineration but that all plastics had to be burnt as close to the low-water mark as possible - otherwise the remnants would not be carried away by retreating waves. Though Andrew and Nelson probably did more than their fair share of rubbish-burning, they were not at all concerned about unburnable refuse and frequently chose a site above high-water mark. I would wait until they had gone off on one of their foraging excursions and then beetle down to the offending location, where I would spend half-an-hour hurling unpleasant bits of eye-sore into the sea. It was extremely unlikely that anybody would land on Inaccessible for at least another five years, by which time all our refuse would be completely obliterated, but this was one of my fads of which nearly everybody approved.

Nearly everybody was less approving about my desire to keep the main Log looking neat and tidy, but then nearly everybody had not spent the best part of three days copying in all the entries from the temporary Log, having to enquire at frequent intervals from both senior and junior members what it was that they had thought they had written. I suggested that we should continue to write up the temporary Log each day before transcribing it; this idea was rejected by a majority of nine to one on the grounds that the Log would not then be so 'spontaneous.' My second suggestion that an exact (but tidier) copy of the original could hardly fail to retain its 'spontaneity' was rejected as 'unscientific.' I surrendered ungraciously and continued to keep up the temporary Log on my own, as a brief record of the day to day happenings, without any of the dramatic passionate intensity or the spine-chilling spontaneity of the main Log ...

If the worst nights described in the Log (and in our private diaries) were those of violent wind when the hut was visibly moving as well as leaking, I think the times when I was most aware of our puny minuteness was when I looked down on the hut from the sheer precipices above. I would shiver with fear at the vertiginous depths, reproach myself for cowardice, thinking of Cressida, who, as Chaucer observes somewhere :

was the ferfullest wight that mighte be.

From there it was only a step to the recollection of 3a's English lesson on 15 September, which made matters so much worse that I had to pretend that I had something in my eye:

And down from thennes faste he gan avyse
This litel spot of erthe, that with the se
Embraced is ...

Food for thought.

CHAPTER 11

'THIS LITEL SPOT OF ERTHE'

La capitale de tout le groupe de Tristan d'Acunha consiste en un petit village situé au fond de la baie sur un gros ruisseau fort murmurant. Il y avait là une cinquantaine de maisons assez propres et disposées avec cette régularité géométrique qui parait être le dernier mot de l'architecture anglaise. Derrière cette ville en miniature s'étendaient quinze cents hectares de plains, bornées par un immense remblai de laves; au-dessus de ce plateau, le piton conique montait à sept mille pieds dans les airs.'

Jules Verne: *Les Enfants du Capitaine Grant*

If the keynotes of the end of the last chapter and the beginning of this one are both fear, the reader will understand why the early afternoon of 30 November found me on my knees in the Church of St Mary, giving thanks for safe delivery and admiring the pulpit which we had brought out from England as the Expedition's gift.

On 24 November, I wrote in my diary:

'We spent the first fortnight of this Expedition worrying about how to get on Inaccessible, the next three weeks twisting our knickers about how we could all stay on Inaccessible and since then (certainly as far as Richard and I are concerned) a great deal of time worrying how we are going to get off! A tremendous swell made all thought of the barge coming impossible, as it did the thought of Andrew and Nelson fishing ...'

Monday, 29 November, will remain indelible in my memory for many reasons, the first two of which are that it typifies the changeability of the weather and the sources of worry detailed in the preceding paragraph.

I was unable to sleep from about 3 am onwards and was feeling very rocky by 5.30 am. I got up at quarter to six and decided to try a mug of Glucodin, of which we had such plenteous unused supplies that I felt no shadow of guilt at helping myself when the others were not present. Astonishingly, it worked. The sea was calm and I fed the troops and did the washing up.

Tristania II, as recounted elsewhere, had been fishing off Inaccessible since the 23rd, and at 8.15 am she sounded her siren, indicating that she wanted to talk to us. We made contact and found that Peter was talking to Tristan who wanted to know what the landing conditions were like. Nelson said they were fine. Peter said he would transmit this to Tristan immediately but he would call again at 10 am to tell us what was happening.

That left a considerable lull, unfortunately unequalled by the sea conditions which gradually became more doubtful. At that stage, only I, Richard Preece and Gilfie, who had been mysteriously ill for some four days, were planning to go to Tristan should the barge arrive and I remember warning the other two not even to start preparing to leave until we had definite word. It duly arrived at about ten past ten when Peter told us that the barge and the launch had left at 9.30 and that we should expect them at around 12.30 pm. By midday the sea conditions were habitually rough with the habitual 12-foot waves, and I served an habitual lunch, during which Nelson expressed a firm view that by now the boats would have turned back. We had all spent some time in the previous hours staring at North Point and Warren's Cliff, around which *Agulhas*, *Hilary*, and *Tristania II* had all come into view on previous occasions. Nick and I had been considerably shaken when Nelson and Andrew had told us that they wished to return on the barges if they arrived - I felt guilty at abandoning Nick with a reduced source of 'land' supplies even though I knew the tinned and dehydrated stocks were more than equal to what we had already consumed (if not so varied). God knows what Nick felt.

By quarter to one lunch was over and we had all accepted Nelson's verdict that the barges had turned back. None the less, the five would-be voyageurs had not unpacked, nor had any of the other members dispersed: we lingered around the outside of the hut, glancing northwards and occasionally southwards to see if 'Tristania II' might be coming back into view. At about ten past one, when we had all given up, Nick suddenly pointed to somewhere near the middle of our horizon and we observed two tiny boats progressing through the swells towards us: once spotted, the activity around the hut became frenetic as Nelson, a skilled helmsman, urged us to have everything ready at the appointed landing-place on the shingle.

The tiny boats drew nearer, the swell increased and we realised that each of the tiny boats was towing an even tinier dinghy and that it was from these that all landings were to be effected. The boats hove to a hundred and fifty yards offshore and the dinghies came plunging towards us, though not before a stray oar had had to be prevented from drifting off towards South America. The young Tristan oarsmen brought in their cargoes of visitors and supplies unhesitatingly and once the dinghies were at knee depth, Nelson led a charge to grab hold of them and haul them up the shingle out of reach of the biggest waves. Colin Redston stepped from the first dinghy, shook my hand and demanded indignantly,

"What the hell did Nelson mean when he said that conditions were all right for landing?"

"At eight-fifteen they were," I told him, suppressing the fact that any one of us could have told him that by lunchtime, they wouldn't be.

In view of the worsening conditions, our visitors, who included the Chief Islander, were in a tearing hurry to get back to sea. They made a perfunctory tour of the hut, helped us to unload supplies and reload our considerable baggage. It occurred to me that it would be a good idea if the three passengers had their passports with them, if they were to pass through South Africa successfully, and these were hurriedly dug out of one of the supply boxes. We made our farewells as Ian took pictures; I stepped into the stern of the first dinghy, clutching my black attaché-case. Timing their effort, a mixed group of Expedition members and islanders relaunched us, the islanders jumping on board at the last moment as the single oarsman deftly propelled the craft through the first breaker at an angle of some sixty-five degrees [*See Plate 16*]. Some ten minutes later I found myself ensconced in the launch (which was on its maiden voyage, having been christened by Marie-José Redston that morning) together with Colin, Chief Islander Albert and half a dozen islanders and expatriates. Fifty yards away the barge was loading the other Expedition passengers and a few minutes later both vessels began to move out to sea, each towing its attendant dinghy. A large wave smashed over the bows of the launch, projecting a waterfall from the coaming over my head and shoulders. I wedged my attaché-case in a locker, wiped my glasses and looked back at the shore. Seven tiny figures stood waving on the shingle and I waved back. Another torrent of water poured over the coaming but this time I decided not to wipe my glasses. I went on waving in the direction where I guessed the figures must be and Colin, with admirable discretion, engaged my immediate neighbours in a conversation about the seaworthy nature of the new boat.

Half an hour late, soaked to the skin, I glanced across at the barge as it wallowed along some sixty yards to starboard. The shiny green oilskins of Nelson and Andrew were clearly visible and Gilfie in his bright blue waterproof waved cheerfully. Automatically I did a count and my heart skipped a beat. Where was the Invertebrate Zoologist? For five minutes I agonised about telling Colin that we seemed to be one member short and then a large roller lifted the barge so high to starboard that I was able to see into her scuppers, where another figure in a bright blue waterproof lay prostrate (the marks on his back were still visible three weeks later).

Gradually the shape of Inaccessible diminished behind us and Tristan loomed mountainously in front. Several times our coxswain was forced to swing the launch to port, to head into waves which threatened to broach us but after about three hours we came level with the south western corner of Tristan and Colin, who had been smiling cheerfully throughout the voyage, shouted that we would be home in about half an hour. I found that my fingers had stiffened into their gripping position on the edge of the coaming and that the water was rising above ankle level in my wellingtons. The barge was now on our port bow and, amazingly, seemed to be progressing on a nearly level course. The Tristan girl at the other end of our boat, who had been sick two hours previously, grinned at me. We overtook two small fishing boats and some twenty minutes later slipped quietly into the little harbour where a large group of people formed a welcoming committee ...

Two days later, I mentioned to Marie-José how frightened I had been during the crossing but how Colin's lack of concern had made me realise that there was no danger. She looked at me in surprise.

"Mais il m'a dit qu'il avait très peur," she said.

On landing in the tiny man-made harbour, Richard and Gilfie were taken off by Richard Grundy, while I was swept away by Marie-José with Colin: I was clutching my precious attaché-case (minus one handle) but I abdicated responsibility for all the rest of our baggage, which duly arrived at the Residency doorstep some two hours later. I didn't even have a chance to say "Goodbye" to Nelson and Andrew who presumably were being reclaimed joyfully by their own: maybe they were responsible for the direction of the luggage because each article arrived at its correct destination, despite the entire absence of labels.

All my clothing was sodden but Marie-José had realised that I was as near size to Colin as made no difference and had equipped me with a complete set of his clothes: more importantly I had the chance of indulging in a hot bath - I was instructed to take as long as I liked because Colin was quite happy with a shower and I took full advantage of the instruction. The comforts of clean (Tristan-made) socks, of dinner at a table, of video-cassette television while seated in an armchair and of a bed with a proper mattress and real sheets all paled into insignificance beside the release from responsibility: at five past midnight on 30 November, I was sitting in bed writing my diary and thinking about Nick and the other six still on Inaccessible and at 3 am I was still awake, despite the fact that I had only slept for four hours the previous night: the settlement of Edinburgh is far enough removed from the shore for the sound of breakers not to carry and I couldn't get used to the silence (this silence is accentuated by the absence of bird calls - in the ensuing week I could count the number of species I observed on the fingers of one hand). I dozed off at about half-past three and at about six I received a visitation from Philip and Peter who were clearly fascinated by my beard. Their mother shooed them away indignantly despite my reassurance that I woke up automatically at 6 am and that anyway I was pleased to receive such visitors.

I don't know how much Richard Preece slept that night but he had been so sick during the crossing from Inaccessible that he probably managed eight hours; as he was staying with Richard Grundy however, he was pressed into the classroom that very morning, while Woolley was still filling Madame Redston's washing-machine with dirty laundry. By lunch I had reorganised both my own and the Expedition's baggage and in the afternoon I visited the School, where I quickly found myself promising to teach an English lesson the following day and to take Assembly and teach all Thursday morning. Any doubts or worries I had had about meeting large numbers of unknown people were quickly dispelled by the friendliness of our reception: apart from my own utility as a teacher, we were valuable as 'new' faces, particularly to the expatriate community. (In fact, the only time I suffered from mass-phobia was at Heathrow Airport nearly three weeks later.)

The weather was much rougher than the previous day: there was no fishing, and as I settled down to packing up some of the thousands of stamp covers which had been entrusted to my care, I thought of the seven remaining explorers who, in those conditions, would probably be occupied preparing some more. At least they now had an oven and had been restocked with food (Nelson and Andrew had been sent enormous individual parcels by their families but had left them behind to add to the supplies.) It being Tuesday, there was no 'sched' with them so I spent half the afternoon finding my way around the settlement. It was easy to fix the location of the main buildings, the School, Prince Philip Hall, the Church, the hospital, the Administration building and the factory, but much more difficult to identify individual dwelling places. Similarly, the main roads were easy but the labyrinth of little paths, composed of cindery volcanic rubble and twisting between the clumps of New Zealand flax and the apparently identical houses was quite another matter, as was the delicate question of whether there was a right of way or was one walking through somebody's garden?

In the course of my visit to the School I had appointed Richard Grundy as our Honorary Social Secretary, a task which he fulfilled with distinction during the following week. The first of my engagements was at six o'clock that evening at his house, which I found unhesitatingly, following an earlier reconnaissance. There I met Richard and Gilfie and was introduced to Harold Green who had originally been designated as one of our guides but who had had to withdraw because one could not be certain that he would be back on Tristan for the wedding of his son, Richard, which had taken place on 25 November (and which he would NOT have been able to attend had he come with us). A former Chief Islander I found it very easy to talk to him and realised that the Expedition's reputation had already been much enhanced by the reports of Nelson and Andrew, who had spent the previous twenty-four hours giving glowing accounts of their experiences. Evidently there was going to be competition for the Expedition guide appointments after Christmas!

Richard had prepared an excellent dinner and we proceeded from his house to our first Tristan birthday party after a short lesson in Tristan 'politesse.'

"Have you got a present for Barbara?" he asked.

I waved an Expedition mug (we had brought two boxes with our crest on) at him.

"Excellent," he said. "You will be offered anything you like to drink but don't ask for anything except brandy or beer; the others are all too expensive. We should not stay for more than an hour, but I'll give you the nod when it's time to go."

We followed him obediently and eventually came to the door of the usual single-story dwelling where we were ushered into a kitchen-cum-living room with an entirely female population. I was introduced to Barbara, congratulated her on her birthday and presented her with an Expedition mug. From there we were conducted to another room where the population was all male and where I was confronted by 'young' h'Arberd, who asked me what I would like to drink. Mindful of my instructions and aware of the harmful effects of beer on the belly, I asked for brandy and was offered a half-pint glass which was three-quarters full of that liquid. Neat. I sipped cautiously, talked to various guests about what we had been doing on Inaccessible and became aware that the lady in whose honour the party was being held was not present. I made my way back to the other room and toasted her, nibbling at the delicious hors d'oeuvres which were scattered about all over the house in profusion.

Some twenty minutes later the Hon. Social Secretary appeared and, having made suitable courteous observations to Barbara and the other ladies present, signified with a lift of his eyebrows that he wanted my attention. Imagining that this was the signal for departure I edged towards him to receive the muttered injunction: "You're in the wrong bloody room!" A moment later he led me into the passage and with an explanatory "That's the women's room" headed back to the all-male population where, some ten minutes later, having been incautious enough to place my nearly empty glass on the floor, I was horrified to find it refilled to its original height. Perhaps I should say terrified, not horrified, but surreptitious use of innocent empty glasses and an unsuspecting pot plant found me ready for the Hon. Social Secretary's next nod, which this time did indicate that departure was now due.

En route back to his house I was informed of further rigueurs of Tristan politesse.

Re-entering his living room, I was pleased to note that the top record on a pile of some thirty discs was something by the Watersons. When I told mine hosts that the perpetrators of that record lived about half a mile from my home, my stock soared - by that stage of the evening, the term is probably irrelevant, but it gave rise to a lot of conversation. We reviewed our efforts on

Inaccessible with our host giving interested support as he did when I eventually showed an interest in going home. As Richard Preece said later, they pointed me in the right direction and hoped for the best. Their hopes were realised even though I wasn't quite sure whether to extinguish the friendly candle in the Residency's corridor ...

Again, it was too quiet to sleep, even after the strains of the evening ...

I confessed my brick to Marie-José at breakfast the following morning.

"J'ai fait un faux-pas," I said.

"Comment?"

"A l'anniversaire de Barbara hier soir - J'ai passé au moins vingt minutes dans la salle de dames à parler avec Barbara et les autres ..."

Marie-José lapsed into English, which she rarely did when I was around.

"Good," she said.

Her animadversions on the patriarchal nature of Tristan society then branched into the social necessity for visiting Auntie Martha Rogers that morning. For my part I felt no necessity, rather a keen desire as I had already been the bearer on my previous visit of a letter from Mike Swales to that lady, an ex-Headwoman of the Island - a fact which I inadvertently mentioned to mine hostess to be rewarded with a fairly Gallic stony glare, the sort of thing they had chosen me for because they obviously knew I was capable of enduring it. Auntie Martha was eighty-six and clearly held the affections of the entire island including the expatriate community because we were joined by Maria Jebb and Bhavina Dave, Maria bringing her two-year old Richard to keep young Peter Redston company.

Apart from the 'Wattle bush' tree in Auntie Martha's garden with its magnificent vermillion flowers, my recollection is of an old lady with incredible generosity of spirit and understanding kindness. We were received in her 'kitchen room' in stately fashion and exchanged conversation amiably but so ineffectually that I came away wishing that I had been able to stay for another couple of weeks ... There was a fracas between the little boys in the garden so their mothers were getting ready to beat the hell out of them - I remember the calm assurance with which Auntie Martha established the eternal verity that kindness was the only essential ingredient in any medicine needed for the curing of the young.

Back at the Residency, Marie-José sat me in a chair in her kitchen and proceeded to cut my hair, avowing that I couldn't possibly teach the 4th form looking like that. She must have done a good job because they listened most attentively to my hastily cobbled together discourse on the importance of language - I had used quotations from Shakespeare and Dickens to illustrate my theme but it is not perhaps irrelevant at this point to quote an extract from my diary during the voyage back to Cape Town some ten days later, when I observed that nobody could possibly understand the *Ode to a Nightingale* until they had read it a thousand miles from land without explanatory notes.

I spent more time in the afternoon preparing the parcels of stamp covers; in the end I sent six large boxes, wrapped in semi-waterproof paper, each with its own Customs declaration ('philatelic material') to myself in North Yorkshire by sea mail. They arrived about three months later, not all together but spaced out over some three weeks: accustomed as I am to the vagaries of the GPO, I sweated that one out myself - there was nobody I could complain to anyway.

Just after half-past three I discovered that my grey anorak was still wet from the crossing forty-eight hours before so I set off to do the 'sched' with Richard Grundy wearing only the Expedition's all wool dark blue pullover. It was a fortunate mischance. We had a couple of miles to cover and we were a little late so Richard strode along energetically using his whole six feet two to advantage while I puffed in his wake doing about two strides to his one. He explained that Richard Preece and Gilfie had both been involved in a rather heavy lunch of stuffed mutton and Tristan pie (known in Yorkshire as Spotted Dick pudding) but that they were hoping to catch us up in time to come in for the end of the 'sched.' We came to the bottom of Hill Piece, the hill from which Inaccessible is visible and from the summit of which Richard was wont to make his regular contact with the Expedition. He indicated the point he wanted to reach and we started climbing ... Ten minutes later, getting no answer to a question I threw over my shoulder, I looked round to find Richard about a hundred yards behind me. Further still below I picked out the figure of the Invertebrate Zoologist but the realisation of my mountaineering prowess was such that I immediately turned away and forged ruthlessly upwards. In the event Richard (Grundy) arrived, as usual dead on time and we talked to Joe, who had been surveying with Clive and who was full of enthusiasm about how they were coping, particularly about how they had 're-organised' the kitchen! The other Richard arrived in time to come in on the end of the conversation, after which he entered into an intense geological discussion with Grundy, surveying strata and volcanological formations from our comfortable seat on the grass of Hill Piece.

That was fine, and I have always been in favour of letting the scientists have their bit of fun but what followed was not funny at all. Those two imbeciles led me and Gilfie on a little walk along the edge of a precipice, gazing solemnly down two hundred metres of sheer cliff face and talking learnedly about stratification and terracing like a couple of aldermanic penguins. Gilfie and I followed dutifully - I think Gilfie was counting sheep and potato patches on the landward side - personally I was three yards to the rear and on all fours! Had we gone through all this to fall off a precipice in a civilised community?

Eventually we got back on to safer bits of mountain from which we descended to the settlement in reasonable order. We separated to our various havens and changed into respectable attire as we were bidden that evening to a reception offered by Richard Green and his bride of six days, Francesca, who was one of the few Islanders I already knew fairly well because she helped Marie-José in the running of the Residency. Armed with a couple of Expedition mugs, we sallied forth and were relieved to be greeted in a room which contained both males and females, though we were embarrassed to discover mountains of food surrounding the wedding-cake, propped against which was a cable of congratulation from the DEI. I muttered instructions to Gilfie and Richard to do their best, while explaining to lovely Francesca that we were dining that evening at the Residency (a fact of which Francesca must have been fully aware but the inexorable laws of Tristan hospitality have to be obeyed). My two companions did a sterling job - I don't think either of them stopped eating for about three days after our landing - and we returned to the Residency at the right time.

My own rapport with Colin and Marie-José had been so instantaneous that I was already inclined to take them for granted: it was an education for me to experience the charm and diplomacy which they could employ in making Richard and Gilfie feel at home and talk about the Expedition; it was equally instructive in that the latter felt free to express opinions which he had certainly never expressed in the confines of the hut. I kept (I hope) suitably quiet and realised that all kinds of things which I had only vaguely suspected to be were genuinely true, or at least were genuinely true in the minds of other people. It was a delicious dinner in exquisitely (I use the word advisedly) civilised surroundings and I don't know whether it has stuck in my mind more for its gastronomic delights than for its philosophic ones. Maybe both: I knew I was putting on weight again and I couldn't have cared less.

The following morning found me very definitely 'on duty' with Richard Preece in support. John Cooper had no hesitation in plonking me in front of the school and telling me to get on with it. I felt terribly nervous but they seemed to listen attentively as I explained what we felt about the importance of Inaccessible. I talked very simply: "Obviously" [*Helpful comment from Invertebrate Zoologist*] about Darwin and emphasised that the Island was their heritage because it was so relatively unspoilt. The introduction of any kind of foreign species would be an ecological disaster, but I am not sure if they took in the latter part of my message. I also told them about the map [*See Plate 4*].

Richard and I then taught Form 3 till break (the lesson lasted an hour and a quarter). This was hard work because I was out of practice and they were preternaturally silent but Richard was very quick to come in when I dried up and only used terms such as 'endemic fauna and flora,' 'lepidoptera,' and 'freshwater invertebrates' once or twice. We made a quick trip to the transmitting shack during break but failed to make contact with Joe at the hut on a different transceiver which, we had hoped, would have made the climb to the top of Inaccessible and the climb to Hill Piece unnecessary. Then back to a combination of Forms 1 and 2, who were much more ready to ask questions and were clearly fascinated by my account of egg-hunting with Andrew, probably for entirely the wrong reasons. Gwynneth Cooper, who was standing in for a sick Island teacher, told us that we had given her material which would last her six weeks and we later received a charming letter of appreciation from Form 1, which was duly pasted into the temporary Log (the latter had been entrusted to my care when the Expedition split up so that there would be a complete record of all our doings). By 12.45 pm I was absolutely shattered but was relieved when Colin suggested that we should now break the habit of a lifetime and have a couple of beers before lunch.

In the afternoon I completed the stamp parcels and sent them all off; Marie-José decided that her efforts on my hair required further treatment so she completed that job and later I wrote letters to various members of my family and close friends, all fairly short because it was a moot point whether I or the letters would arrive home the soonest.

I had been given a rendez-vous of 1900 hours in the Hon Social Secretary's house, whence we proceeded to Bennie's birthday party. Here we were somewhat confused to find both sexes in the same room. The only expatriate lady was immediately identifiable because she was the only one not knitting: I was introduced to Libby, the wife of the Agricultural Officer, Stiubhard, who had been among the visitors to Inaccessible the previous Monday. It emerged that we were to be fellow-guests at the Residency dinner later that evening and that we were to be fellow-passengers on the *Tristania II* whenever Peter Warren decided that conditions were suitable for embarkation.

If I had some difficulty in sorting out the expatriate community, the enormous ramifications of inter-relationships among the Islanders became clear as a result of that evening. I had already visited the Council Chamber in the Administrative block and had seen the separate charts for the seven families, each family having a separate colour. The population is now around three hundred and in his book *Tristan da Cunha and the Roaring Fifties*, Allan Crawford, FRGS[43] has shown how a brother and sister who descended from the original settlers can be shown to be related to each other fifty-six times over. One Tristan custom which had evolved among the expatriates, and which is followed as inexorably as the customs of the Islanders, is that an expatriate 'going home' is invited to dinner by the Administrator and he can ask any two couples from among the Islanders as fellow-guests. In this case Stiubhard and Libby had chosen Ernest and Daphne Repetto and Cheseldon and Janet Lavarello: they were introduced to me as Arnie and Daphne and Ches and Jeanette, and we had a splendid evening which was particularly enlivened by Arnie's descriptions of past visits to Inaccessible and Nightingale: Arnie and Ches are the kind of men described in Hervé Bazin's *Les bienheureux de la Désolation* in the following terms:
Métis de rescapés, à vingt couleurs, tous anglo-dano-américano-italo-hottentots, tous à la fois marins, bergers, paysans, montagnards, habitués aux rigueurs, aux privations, aux accidents, trouvant tout naturel de chasser pour le bifteck le taureau sauvage du versant sud ou d'expédier leur fils chercher des oeufs d'oiseau pour l'omelette familiale sur les îlots voisins, par des vagues de trois mètres.

However, when I came to work out the surnames of these friendly people nineteen months later, I spent two hours poring over the Tristan family tree and ended up telephoning Mike Swales three times in one morning to see if he could help as the problems continued to multiply! Stiubhard and Libby were not going home in the happiest of circumstances following a disagreement with the Administrator, but this was something which I did not realise until about a week later so there was the occasional awkward silence which I couldn't understand in such an entertaining and interesting evening.

Then I started to write a long letter to Nick in the hope of bringing him up to date straight after his arrival on Tristan with the rest of the Expedition. I managed a couple of pages of foolscap before I finally gave up and I must have been writing by candlelight because it wasn't a fishing day. My knowledge of Tristan's problems and of Tristan lore was increasing every day; I was torn between my desire to warn Nick about possible pitfalls and my anxiety to get down all the things which I had experienced. I knew, for example, that Arnie and Ches were direct descendants of two Italian sailors who had been shipwrecked on Tristan from the barque *Italia* in 1892; I knew that Nelson and Harold were descendants of a Dutchman called Groen who had been shipwrecked from the schooner *Emily* in 1836; I knew that the low-lying promontory on which we had built our hut on Inaccessible was named Blenden Hall after an East Indiaman which had been wrecked there in 1821. The true effect of the way in which storm and shipwreck are deeply interwoven into the life and traditions of the Tristan Islanders was only brought home to me, however, when I walked into a dwelling-place and saw the name 'Mabel Clark' carved in large letters along one of the crossbeams at the gable end of the living-room. The barque *Mabel Clark* (how could anybody call a barque Mabel Clark?) had been wrecked in 1878 and a hundred years later her timbers were still serving as essential portions of homes on the Island. None of this got into my letter to Nick, which was of a much more pragmatic nature; what I tried to convey was the helpful and friendly attitude to the Expedition which I was meeting everywhere and it would be disingenuous of me not to admit that this was a welcome surprise after some of the disappointments of the previous eight weeks.

I suppose that life on Tristan was somewhat mundane after the rigours of Inaccessible; if this chapter conveys a sense of mundaneity, the intention is quite deliberate. On the Friday morning, it gave me great pleasure to go and talk to Professeur Redston's two students of French (both expatriate children who would have to study the language when they went to school in the UK). They were intelligent and Marie-José had obviously given them a good grounding but it was only after spending half the lesson overcoming their shyness that I was able to help a little bit, mainly with suggestions of further lessons. Meanwhile Richard Preece had gone bug-hunting with some of Richard Grundy's class and Gilfie had again disappeared with some of the Agricultural Officer's forces. Returning to the Residency for mid-morning coffee, we discovered that Colin had received a telex to the effect that RP and I were booked on a South African Airways flight from Cape Town to London on 18 December. Bernard Hill, our invaluable Old Denstonian linkman, obviously had a sublime belief in the inalterability of *Tristania II*'s sailing date and ETA (neither of which we knew): my own experience of the South Atlantic up to then led me to express considerable reservations but there was nothing we could do about it.

'Tristan, c'est comme la vie: on sait quand on y entre, Dieu seul sait quand on en sort ...'

If my activities in the afternoon were again somewhat domestic, they were nonetheless enjoyable both for me and for other members of the Expedition, whether on Tristan or Inaccessible. It had become clear at lunch that Philip Redston was not at all well, so while his mother took him off to see Dr. Naredna Dave at the hospital, I sat with young Peter which was some entertainment for me though it may have cramped his style a little. I have already commented on my value as a new face in my account of my first full day on Tristan: on that afternoon I had been visited by Bhavina Dave and greeted with a warmth which was flattering from such a beautiful young woman, though Marie-José quickly made it clear that neither my youth, charm nor intelligence even existed and that my novelty would quickly wane ... I was therefore delighted (and flattered) by the speedy arrival of Maria Jebb on this later date (particularly as she took charge of the latter end of a rather protracted session on the pot from young Peter) though I realised the extent of, and restrictions on, my duties (tea and sympathy?) We had a long conversation about the difficulties of life in such isolation and my own insistence on the uniqueness of their luck was refuted as it usually was on similar occasions. Maria hailed from Colombia, Marie-José from Paris, Naredna and Bhavina originally from Kenya, Stiubhard from Scotland and Michael the Padré from South Africa, so the extraordinary blend of racial origin in the Tristan Islanders' make-up was reflected in the expatriate community in December 1982. At least a quarter of those would be departing at the same time as Richard and me on the *Tristania II* and their replacements would be Islanders which was right and proper ... but the numbers in the School were declining ... Who would be there when HMG decided that one teacher for an age-range of 6-15 was enough? I explained to Maria that it was quite clear to me that the Island needed two teachers with contrasting degrees and qualifications, apart from the unqualified Island teachers, whatever the numbers in the School. Only thereby would Tristan continue to progress as a self-supporting community, which, astonishingly, at that time, it was.

I had to leave early for the 'sched' because I had young Peter in his push-chair. The cold, bright rush of South Atlantic wind soon dispelled any forebodings or gloomy thoughts. On my right the gulches descended to the ocean, full of rubbish and refuse, though there were certain green patches on the slopes above which indicated vaguely the location of the Tristan Golf Course, presumably the most exclusive Golf Club in the world. Various Islanders passed me in both directions, mostly on foot or with donkeys but there was one car and one tractor. Nevertheless we were rather solitary until we came to the point where the push-chair was no longer viable. We put it safely in a convenient ditch and I put Peter on my shoulders.

"Now we're going up Hill Piece," I said.

"Gerrup," he said.

I 'gorrup' and met Richard, who had been doing something

geological, at the appointed place and we duly made contact with Joe on Inaccessible. No doubt we transmitted the important bits of information (I think that was the day when they reported that they couldn't find the Cape Gooseberry) and no doubt Preece and Gilfie materialised at the right moment (they must have done because I have a precious photo of Peter sitting on my shoulders in that location) - nonetheless, my recollection of the 'sched' is of people rolling around on tops of their respective mountains as it became apparent that my own transmissions were being interrupted by the two-year-old who was sitting on my shoulders. Knowing, or thinking that we knew, the exigencies of South Atlantic intercourse, the Invertebrate Zoologist and I bade the Expedition farewell again, wishing them luck again before our departure. Perhaps the full implications of our sailing or of our exertions on behalf of the Expedition were beginning to impinge even on to Inaccessible because Joe sounded almost lachrymose - certainly our farewells and good wishes were accepted with feeling.

We retraced our steps rather thoughtfully and, in my case, very carefully.

Then I completed the other half of my letter to Nick before rejoining the others chez Grundy. Here we met Andrew, whom I had not seen since our landing - I had only encountered Nelson twice and in each case somewhat momentarily - we had so much to talk about that we were rather late for our dinner with John and Gwynneth Cooper. Luckily there were still busy coping with putting their four children to bed and Woolley ended up reading a bedtime story to Neil and then singing the whole of 'A partridge in a pear-tree' in a duet with him for the benefit of his little sister Joy.

Conversation at dinner again turned to the problems of the Islanders - even though the community was self-supporting at that time, philately supplied more of its income than the famous crayfish which were in danger of being over-fished, moreover there seemed to be a falling birth-rate which conflicted with the dangers of in-breeding - and I suppose it was a tribute to the warmth of their family feeling that the problems of the expatriates hardly cropped up in the conversation: John and Gwynneth were so serene and secure in their faith that when their mid-term three month leave came round, they only spent ten days of it in the UK because they were anxious not to miss the next boat returning to Tristan.

I came back to the Residency to find a bridge quartet in progress, Colin and Marie-José having invited Chris and Maria Jebb for that purpose. I suspect that the ladies had got together a little earlier in order to plan a picnic excursion to the annual sheep-shearing which, weather permitting, was due to take place the following day. If their husbands seemed to have slight reservations, I was all in favour, as I knew that nobody else from the Expedition would have this opportunity so I volunteered my services as a porter either of children or supplies. The sheep-shearing site was beyond the potato patches and was therefore some three and a half miles distant.

Philip and Peter arrived in my room to make sure I was awake at 6.15 the next morning, by which time Gilfie had probably already departed to the flocks with Chief Shepherd Andrew. The two Richards had hatched their own plot to climb to 'Base,' the first plateau at about five hundred metres up the mighty walls, so clearly my own duty was to make a photographic record of the sheep-shearing, particularly as the weather was fine and bright. Colin discovered that he had a cipher message to decode but the rest of us set off at about half-past nine, me, Marie-José and her two small boys, Chris and Maria with their little girl and even younger boy, and Naredna and Bhavina Dave. Each of the wives had provided a different part of the picnic whose dimensions made us bear a distinct resemblance to those Sherpa porters in pictures of Himalayan expeditions in the 1920's, and I quickly appreciated the importance of Colin's cipher message. We made our way slowly along the metalled road which extended at least half the way to our destination and with which I was quite familiar as I had already used it twice on my way to Hill Piece. Most of the Islanders had preceded us though we were overtaken by one or two small groups and even met people who were already returning home. We gossiped in different groups and I loaded myself with a tired child as well as an extra haversack in a deliberate effort to slow myself down -shades of Clive going up Inaccessible! As we came round the corner of Hill Piece and crossed Big Sandy Gulch, we saw the mass of sheep about three-quarters of a mile in front of us and, amazingly, some twenty miles beyond, Inaccessible for once was clearly visible: we had not been able to see it during either of our 'scheds' from the top of Hill Piece.

The annual sheep-shearing on Tristan was not an event of which the Agricultural Officer approved, as was demonstrated by his absence on this occasion. Each householder is permitted to graze a certain number of sheep which carry his individual mark and all the animals were instantly recognisable by the shepherds, particularly our own Andrew. The pasturage was heavily overgrazed, as was evidenced by the meagre size of some of the animals. They had apparently been herded by their respective owners all at the same time in one mass collection, during which one's main concern was to get one's own flock into the family pen without getting trampled in the stampede. By the time we arrived, much of the resultant earlier chaos had, according to Gilfie, died down: it had produced three or four serious accidents which had condemned the unfortunate animals to the family pot but as various other uninjured beasts had clearly been selected for the same fate, nobody apart from the Agricultural Officer seemed very worried. The men were now engaged in the shearing process and the product of their efforts was entirely typical of what is expected from the average Tristan male. Some of the shorn sheep were being released in a state of overall pure white nudity, their owners' initials neatly and clearly stamped in red or blue on their flanks. Others, like the thatched roof of Dylan Thomas' small, unhappy public house (*The Mountain Sheep*) resembled a 'wig with ringworm;' while still others looked as if their owners had made ineffectual dabs at reclaiming chunks of wool from their bodies before dragging the animals through a hedge backwards in order to harvest the rest: the absence of hedges fortunately precluded this possibility.

Each Islander did his own sheep because each Islander was expected to be able to do his own sheep, as he was expected to be able to carve the blocks of 'tuff' (volcanic lava) to build the walls of his house, to cultivate his own potatoes, to fish his own crayfish and Five Finger, to build his own fishing-boat and to avoid shooting his neighbour when hunting the wild cattle on Stonyhill. The women were no less self-sufficient and though I did not spot anybody actually spinning wool on the shearing site, I was delighted to photograph two ladies busily knitting. The other typical feature of this Tristan occasion was that apart from the unavoidably detained (Colin appeared very jauntily about three-quarters of an hour after our arrival) like some people in the factory or the very aged, everybody was there and everybody was looking after the small children. Each time that I looked up to see where Peter had got to or what had happened to little Joy Cooper, I would see some entirely competent twelve-year old seating them on a donkey or some grave matriarch escorting them solemnly away from some source of potential danger.

As lunchtime drew nearer the activity declined and many groups disappeared towards their huts on the potato patches while others found convenient sheltered hollows, as we did, to rest and picnic. The combined efforts of our ladies had produced a meal of such astonishing and delicious variety that we all felt fairly somnolent at its conclusion; young Peter promptly went to sleep on his blanket and the rest of us sat contentedly in the sunshine as the few remaining flocks were released to wander free on their treacherous pastures. Knowing the length of the route back, I suddenly noticed that the departure of a tractor was imminent. There were only seven children on the trailer.

"What about these two?" I asked, holding up Peter and Philip.

"Pile "em on," came the answer, and a thirteen-year old who had been a baby-sitter at the Residency on some earlier occasion took them firmly in charge. They departed, ecstatic, though Colin and I then had to spend some time reassuring their mother.

With over three hundred inhabitants, birthday parties occurred several times a week on Tristan. That evening it was the Padré's and it took place earlier than usual, partly because Mrs. Edwards was expecting an addition to the family at any moment and partly because there was to be a dance in Prince Philip Hall to honour the departure of Stiubhard, familiarly known as 'the farmer.' Having congratulated the Padré on behalf of the Expedition, I repaired as usual to the Hon Social Secretary's domain just as he and the Invertebrate Zoologist returned triumphantly from their tour of 'Base.' I was delighted for the latter, who had taken several photographs even though he had found very few *Tristania*, the island snail which, along with another variety called *Succinia* were his particular delectation (neither variety were edible). I was also slightly jealous because Harold Green had approached Colin at the sheep-shearing and indicated that he thought that a tour of the Peak for expatriates was a possibility the following day: as the three DEI members had been booked for lunch with Nelson and dinner with Andrew, there was no way that we could participate and I realised how rare were such chances because Colin himself, though he had been there for a year, had not yet made the ascent.

Richard Grundy generously offered me a copious pot-luck dinner, after which I went back to the Residency to write a final entry for the Main Log, in which Nick had promised to leave a couple of blank pages at the appropriate place. This took me some time and I finished only just before the electricity went off, after which I escorted Marie-José to the dance, as Colin was feeling slightly off-colour and wanted to reserve his forces for the next day's climb. Richard and Gilfie had joined the dance much earlier and Gilfie had already endeared the Expedition more closely to Tristan hearts by participating in the Pillow Dance. This is kind of a Conga (?) (this dance is not in Oxford English Dictionary) in which the first man places a cushion at the feet of the girl of his choice; they kneel and kiss; the girl rises with the cushion and the man tags on behind her as she weaves her way to the man that she would like to kiss, before whom the cushion is placed, after which the appropriate ceremony is repeated. The chosen man then picks up the cushion and sets off in search of the lady of his choice with the first couple tagging on behind and the snake-like dance gradually lengthens until it becomes totally unmanageable and breaks up into hoots of merriment. When Gilfie played his part, the roar could be heard throughout the settlement.

As Marie-José and I entered, we were greeted by the amazing spectacle of what looked like the entire population aged between six and seventy-six gyrating animatedly in half darkness. A man appeared out of the shadows, grabbed Marie-José without so much as 'by your leave' and disappeared with her into the whirling mass. I saw the familiar face of Andrew by the wall, sidled up to him and we talked until the dance ended. My partner made her way back to me as all the ladies scattered to the chairs on the periphery of the hall: all the men congregated in the middle. The music for the next dance started and suddenly the central mass broke up into solitary predators who loomed up without warning, grabbed their chosen prey and redeparted into the maelstrom. I grabbed Marie-José and precipitated ourselves therein while she enlightened me further on Tristan social customs. No doubt I adapted too slowly because having escorted my partner in the custom of my youth, if I was not dancing with her I was usually too late to find a partner because everybody else was already on the floor - except Andrew who, unaccountably, remained by the wall though I knew he had a reputation as an excellent dancer. (I learnt later that a bereavement in his close (!) family laid an embargo by Tristan custom on his participation for a certain period ...) At one point I recognised Daphne just after Marie-José had been seized and I danced with her but on the next occasion when I was partnerless I was apostrophised by a delightful plump young lady called Gillian, telling me "You mustn't be shy" and bringing me engagingly closely into the throng ... Several members of the community had clearly had a few too many ('a bit touch up') but nobody would hold it against them on the morrow: in such a closed society one has to be tolerant and tolerance in the Tristan community seemed to be innate. My final vision was of Richard in the last dance, closely held by a beautiful girl about whom Marie-José muttered direful prophesies as we walked home in almost complete darkness. In normal circumstances I would have taken her arm but on Tristan there might have been a furore.

Next morning, Colin and Marie-José were up at 6 am and I found no difficulty in getting up to help - the smugness of this comment will be reflected in the narration of the events of the late morning and early afternoon. It took some time for them to get ready but by 7.15 they were on their way, leaving me in charge of Philip and Peter, who both behaved beautifully in the absence of their parents. I deposited them with Harold's wife, Amy, at the appointed time, which was too late for me to attend Matins so I came back to get on with more paper-work. Then I made a determined effort to sort out the rest of my kit and took a sack of surplus equipment to the Hon Social Secretary's establishment where the proprietor was (just) up and about but where the Invertebrate Zoologist was still somnolent so I had to shout at him to make clear what I was depositing.

When I got back to my room at the Residency, I continued writing until a knock at the door revealed an aged male who, he said, had come to thank me for saving Nelson's life. As Nelson had probably frequently saved mine, I found it difficult to comprehend what my visitor was on about until he informed me that Colin normally gave him a brandy at this time of day. I obliged him while we chatted about our adventures on Inaccessible but felt it necessary to indicate that the supplies were not inexhaustible when the unknown guest wanted the second half ... He departed, only semi-satisfied. I finished my writing and set off to Nelson's house.

The first person I met was the Invertebrate Zoologist who looked at me vaguely, realised he had seen me somewhere before and asked me why I had woken him up in the middle of the night. When it emerged that the party in Richard Grundy's house after the dance had broken up at 4 am, I felt some sympathy. I was introduced to Winnie, Nelson's wife, and reintroduced to Jack, their son, who had been instrumental in effecting our evacuation from Inaccessible. As Nelson's two godsons and my previous visitor were also present, and as each of the three young men had a lady-in-waiting, there were rather a lot of us in Winnie's kitchen until Nelson solved the problem by moving all the males into the dining-room, where he seated us in all the available chairs. The meal of Tristan stuffed mutton which followed was of gargantuan proportions, though at one moment Nelson noticed something missing. He rapped on the table. Winnie appeared from the kitchen.

"Jawn's got no carrots," said her lord and master, reproachfully.

Winnie disappeared and a moment later one of the ladies in waiting arrived with another bowl of carrots. I meditated on the probable reaction of Sylvie or Marie-José to such an exchange and shuddered.

The meal went on for about two and a half hours and towards the end we managed to bring the sexes together and I took a group photograph in Nelson's garden. As we left, he gave me back my attaché case on which he had sewn two new handles: they have lasted ever since.

I got back to the Residency at about 4 pm. No sign of Colin and Marie-José, who had been due back at 2. Hurriedly I made my way to Harold's house where Philip and Peter were rampaging around a tranquil Amy, who calmly told me that the climbers were just coming off 'the volcano' meaning the eruption of 1961. Sure enough, they walked in about ten minutes later, having had a splendid day but having been delayed by Naredna Dave who had pulled a muscle. On returning home, I borrowed a Prayer-book and made my way to Evensong. There was a rather sparse attendance but Richard Preece slipped in beside me at the last moment and my praises to God were that much more heartfelt because the service differed not one iota from the Evensong of my youth and I had no need of the Prayer-book. The homely nature of Tristan society was impressed on us when the Padré started his sermon by saying how pleased he was to see John and Richard among the congregation. This was not a veiled reproach for our absence from Matins because he already knew that I had been baby-sitting and must have guessed that RP wouldn't have known where he was at that time of morning.

Dinner at Andrew's was a repeat performance of lunch and by 10.15 I was in grave danger of falling asleep. I waddled home feeling as if I wouldn't need to eat for a week to find my hosts frantically writing letters by candlelight.

The 'dong' to signal a 'fishing day' went at 5.30 the following morning, Monday 6 December, and I joined Colin and Marie-José at 6 o'clock to find them finishing their letters, though I think that they had been to bed for a few hours since I had last seen them. Francesca arrived with a pair of Tristan socks for me and a few minutes later Mary, the other Residency assistant, brought my total collection to fourteen pairs! I had remembered that it would be my youngest's birthday on the 10th, so I walked down to the Post Office with Marie-José and Philip to arrange a telegram for him. Suddenly, Philip said "There's a ship!"

Tristania II was coming round the headland and equally suddenly, things started to move fast.

John Cooper had asked me to present Gymnastic Certificates in Assembly at 9 o'clock and I was doubly pleased to do so because it gave me a chance to say farewell. The children sang as they always do, with real enthusiasm and there was a lump in my own throat as I left them: the atmosphere was too like my own school. Then the message came that passengers were due to embark at 12 noon and I managed to catch Gilfie, accompanied by his lady-in-waiting. Gilfie had taken only five days to turn into a right little male chauvinist Tristan pig, having been heard to enquire indignantly on the morning of Saturday the 4th, "Rosemary, why hasn't my shirt been ironed?" ... I asked him to go and make sure that Richard knew what was happening which he immediately promised to do. My own packing didn't take long because I had been gradually discarding useless impedimenta. Colin turned up and we decided to break a further lifetime habit and have a beer before noon: in the end we had a couple before walking down to the harbour for the Tristan farewell - kisses for all the women, handshakes for all the men, half of us fighting back tears, the other half in tears ... There is something terribly final about leaving that

Island and neither Richard nor I could find words to say even to Colin, Marie-José and Gilfie, never mind Nelson and Andrew who were standing on the embarkation quay with tears streaming down their faces. Large numbers of Islanders came out to *Tristania II* to say a last goodbye to Stiubhard and Brian and their families, so Richard and I had time to pull ourselves together in the tiny cabin which we had been allotted almost next door to the Captain's quarters, where we could hear the guests enjoying his hospitality. I walked on to the deck outside our porthole and looked back at the settlement, first with the naked eye and then through binoculars.

CHAPTER 12

END GAME

*O litus vita mihi dulcius, O mare! felix cui licet ad terras ire
subinde meas*   Petronius.
*O sea shore sweeter to me than life, O sea, happy am I who may
come at last to my own lands.*

The naked eye revealed something which I had never seen
before: the settlement of Edinburgh, Tristan da Cunha, from the
sea. If this was a new experience, that is only another apposite
comment on South Atlantic weather. The sheltered side of the
Island used to have a natural harbour as well as a reasonably safe
anchorage until the eruption of 1961: now the sloping walls of the
great volcanic mountain towered before me, the black mass of the
eruption dominating the left-hand side of the settlement. I homed
in to the settlement and picked out the Residency, where two small
figures stood beside the front door - I couldn't tell if they were
waving but I felt a bit like Sir Patrick Spens when he received the
King's letter when walking on the strand. If their figures were
minute, the 1961 eruption was dwarfed by the seven thousand foot
immensity of the mountain, and I traversed the great cliffs with my
binoculars, settling them first on 'Base,' two and a half thousand
feet up ...[*See Plate 17*].
I wandered on upwards and caught a glimpse of the peak,
before coming back to the familiar trail up the valley. Hill Piece
standing green on the right in contrast to the bleakness of the
majestic walls of ugly black lava. There in the forefront was the
factory and beyond it the disabled wind generator (another one but
five times the size of ours!) and beyond that, as I traversed further
right, Inaccessible Island, about two metres to the right of
Hottentot Point. I blew my nose, gulped and took some pictures.
Richard appeared and flung me a can of beer. I gulped again. He
flung me another can and I felt much better.
People were departing (half Tristan seemed to have been on

Leaving Inaccessible

Tristan da Cunha

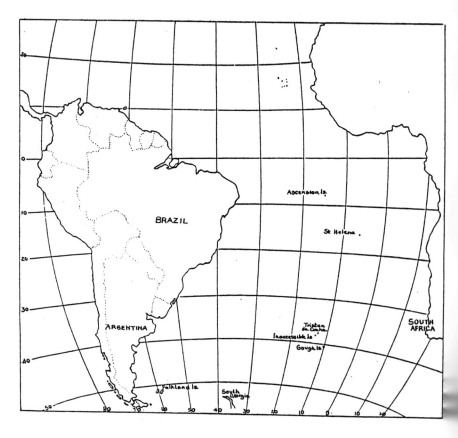

Relative positions.

the boat) and it was touch and go whether *Tristania II* was not swamped from internal precipitation which had nothing to do with the prodigious beer consumption and which continued after sailing time until about 2.30 pm, when Libby Kerr-Liddell guided me knowledgeably down to the dining-room. There we enjoyed delicious fresh bread and cheese, knowing that the ship was moving away from Tristan and knowing that neither of us wanted to look back. Stiubhard and Peter Warren had had a confrontation about what Stiubhard regarded as an unjust distribution of the very limited number of cabins available, a distribution in which Richard and I had come off well (we didn't know it) but with which we had had nothing to do.

Libby shared her extensive knowledge of *Tristania II* (this was her fifth voyage) and I made further first-hand acquaintance with the Captain a little later when, feeling restless, I ventured out into the bows as we came closer to Inaccessible and immediately received an imperious summons from the bridge.

"You are to come on to the bridge any time you want," said the Captain.

My previous experiences led me to take a little time to realise that he meant what he said but once I got the message, I took full advantage of his invitation.

On this first occasion I was overwhelmed by the profusion of bird species that I had missed, not just during the week on Tristan but also on Inaccessible. Apart from the shearwaters, the Mollys, the Stormies and a Wanderer, suddenly there were Pintados and Stinkers as well. I made observations which I recorded on all kinds of scraps of paper, including my cheque-book, but by 4.15 I had been invited down to the Captain's cabin, where he was listening in to a conversation between Joe on Inaccessible and Gilfie on Tristan - a conversation in which we couldn't join because we were out of their line of sight, being moored in the lee of Inaccessible, off Tom's Beach. Some time later, Captain Peter got through to Major Peter in Robin Hoods Bay and I heard that all was well at home. As I felt very well myself, j'en fus assez content, I was even, momentarily, overcome. Only momentarily.

though Captain Peter had insisted on telling Major Peter, mainly for Colonel Sylvie's benefit, that I had lost well over a stone in weight but was 100% fit. At that stage he might even have been right ...

I learnt that we were to fish until Thursday, after which the voyage back to Cape Town would begin.

I don't remember what time I went to bed but I know I didn't sleep very much because my bunk seemed even narrower than my Inaccessible (!) bunk - Richard was delighted because at least the bunks were very long and he had had great difficulty in accommodating his six foot plus prior to this voyage.. By 6 am on the 7th, I had had enough and I went and did some bird-watching on the bridge before descending to the dining-room early so that I could write up some Log before all the small children arrived for breakfast (there was absolutely no space for writing in our cabin and very little for reading). I couldn't resist the bacon and eggs on the breakfast menu - neither could RP who, having consumed his very fair share, retired precipitately to bed because the sea was cutting up decidedly rough. I was able to admire the seamanship and the professional skills of the fishermen on *Tristania II* for the next three hours - apart from the heavy swell there was a patchy fog but each line of traps was duly picked up in sequence, hauled, emptied and passed back through the bowels of the ship, before being recast into the ocean from the stern.

I began to learn my way through the different companionways, corridors, exits and entrances of the ship. I also began to learn how to recognise the different faces of Inaccessible as the island emerged through the mist, and to know which area was, inadvertently, in view. On that morning we were fishing far off South West Point and were probably out of view because the Expedition didn't try to call us, even though we were open to a call from 'Hilary' which was approaching from Nightingale. They too had had poor catches, which I suppose was some consolation to Peter and his crew: the gigantesque proportions of the lunch would have consoled anybody for anything.

In the afternoon Redvers, the first mate, showed me round the 'factory' part of the ship, all of which was in the forward section. The crayfish catch goes in only three directions: whole cooked tails go to the USA, whole cooked crayfish to France, whole uncooked crayfish to Japan, all deep frozen. I watched the crew operating the different procedures and wondered why the French, as usual, had latched on to a delicious source of nutrition which was basically under British control but to which our own marketeers seemed to have no access. The ship moored in the same anchorage as the previous night and Redvers kindly lent me a fishing-line. I never used it because I was anxious to catch up on paperwork and after that day I never had another chance: I felt increasingly virtuous as I worked on my reports because RP had staggered off to watch a video film.

By 5.30 Peter was on the air and very quickly had Peter Walker coming through loud and clear from North Yorkshire. What happened next has never ceased to amaze me as to the speed and efficiency of amateur methods of communication, bearing in mind that we were sitting out in the Atlantic 2000 miles from Cape Town and 8000 miles from home. In all innocence, I asked Peter to ask Peter if he knew who would be meeting me at Heathrow in eleven days time.

Within minutes, as I sat sipping a beer and still not quite able to credit that the voice coming through the loud speaker was that of my friend in Robin Hoods Bay, came the reply, "Mike Swales and John's daughter, Alison." How the news was obtained, I don't even attempt to know. Perhaps Peter already knew and what kind of noun is 'news' anyway? Alistair Cooke recounts the story of some eager editor telegraphing one of his reporters, "Are there any news?" to receive the retort, "Not a new." The speed at which I seemed able to get the odd 'new' from all those many thousand miles away still leaves me amazed - but I couldn't decide where I stood in Mike Swales' popularity stakes, that he should take time, and Alison, to go to London especially to greet the wanderers' return.

I recorded a Kerguelen Petrel and some Sooty Shearwaters before coming to grips with a dome-headed white gull sitting on the water which Peter Warren didn't know about, and neither did I. (I still don't.) Then I accounted for a five-course dinner and started to talk to Stiubhard about his experience on Tristan.

I had been telling him about my own first experience of Tristan hospitality at Barbara's birthday party, with the risk of becoming 'touched up' when piled with glasses of raw brandy, only for Stiubhard to correct me in Tristan Common Usage:

"Not 'touched up,' John. 'Touch up.'"

"Please explain," I said, in my best pedagogic fashion.

"You must understand," he replied, equalling my own pedantic tone, "that only the present tense exists in Tristan common parlance, if one has had a few too many, one is not 'a bit touched up;' one is and one remains 'a bit touch up.' There is a map,' he continued learnedly, 'which records one part of Tristan as 'Down where the Minister landed his things." Totally wrong. It should be "Down where the Minister land his things." The same map gets "Ridge where the goat jump off right," he added condescendingly.

We moved on to pronunciation and the Tristan habit of putting an 'h' in front of words beginning with a vowel and I was moved to tell him the story of Nelson and Andrew's 'hoars,' which was well-received. Stiubhard reminisced about his experiences in the last eighteen months, the most hair-raising of which was the wild cattle shoot at Stony Hill at the southern end of the island, a shoot which, it became clear, was infinitely more dangerous for the hunters than for the hunted as .303 bullets flew in all directions and as the hunters defended themselves from attack. His affection for the hislanders came over in everything he said but most clearly in his account of a recent event when two public works employees had set out to paint a large roof, starting from opposite ends and eventually meeting in the middle, with no means of descent! By the time they got there, word had got round and three-quarters of the population had assembled to see what would happen next ...

I got back to the cabin late but spent some time outside it, standing on the deck, listening to the night noises and looking at the partly visible walls of Inaccessible above Tom's Beach: even though we were well protected from the prevailing winds, there was still a considerable sea running.

Apart from learning my way around the ship and finally realising that I was welcome on the bridge at any time of the day or night - on that occasion it was 4 am because I couldn't sleep - I began to learn my way around the complexities of *Tristania II*'s menus on 8 December. For breakfast, apart from the statutory fruit juice and cereals, I could have worked my way that morning through haddock, bacon and eggs, pork chops and corned beef with chips. Luckily there was toast to fill up with. Lunch started with split-pea soup, followed by cabbage breedie with rice - 'breedie' is an immensely filling kind of fricassée to which I took an immediate liking but it is so filling that the only other courses were a dessert and cheese and biscuits. By dinner time the chef had pulled himself together again and we were able to start with sugar bean soup and follow it up with crayfish mayonnaise (three crayfish each) plus salad. We were allowed to choose between fried Snoek or fried Bluefish for the fish course, which set us up nicely for the braised kidneys and the braised beef which, together with their potatoes, carrots, peas and beans, formed the pièce de résistance. My only excuse for the way I ate on that voyage is that I was averaging about five hours sleep a night: I felt that I would never have such an experience again and I was determined to make the most of it. The generosity and kindness of Peter Warren enabled me to do so: it was on this day that, when I casually mentioned at 7 am that I was going down to the galley to do some writing before the small children arrived, I was told to make free use of the Captain's cabin whenever I wanted to write.

I spent the morning on the bridge. The weather was much calmer than the previous day but we learnt on the radio that there was no fishing from Tristan. Towards lunchtime we decided to stir up the lads and moved in on Blenden Hall sounding the siren. Peter had been showing me some of his old charts and I was able to pass on some information to Clive about the true position of Pyramid Rock and the shape of South Hill. I told them to call us the next day but said another goodbye and good luck just in case. Soon after lunch we anchored off Waterfall as a change from

Tom's Beach. The sea was calm but there was a steady drizzle which discouraged us from fishing. *Hilary* arrived to pick up some electrical gear as we were due to depart the following day and I took some photographs. Then I retired to the Captain's cabin as per instruction and started to draw up endless lists for Mike Swales. There was no sound of the 4.15 Inaccessible - Tristan 'sched' but the cloud was so low that maybe they didn't try. Despite the drizzle, it was very hot on board so I tried to read while the others were watching a rather violent video film. There was an enormous raft of Great Shearwaters just next to the ship making that unforgettable noise; I wondered if I would ever hear it again and underlined the instruction to Mike to bring a tape-recorder. Then I sat up with Richard and Stiubhard exchanging further reminiscences over a convivial glass of Stiubhard's native brew. Later still we caught a Wilson's Storm Petrel and two Diving Petrels which we examined before relaunching them into the boundless South Atlantic night.

Whether it was exhaustion or Stiubhard's potations, I didn't wake until about a quarter past six but then speedily removed to the shower before the ladies started floating about. This, I discovered, was the ideal time to use the shower-room as it enabled one to nip in smartly wearing nothing but a towel and then return to one's cabin to dress, instead of having to balance on the loo pedestal avoiding two or three inches of water sloshing about on the floor. I joined Peter on the bridge as the first line of traps was being brought in for the last time; we were far out to the south-west of Blenden Hall and we waited all morning for a call from the Expedition but they must have been conserving batteries. Peter decided to return round the east side of Inaccessible, bringing the ship in very close to South Hill (too damn close in my view but I managed to avoid asking the Captain if we weren't getting rather near) so that I could see the cave which passed underneath it, appreciate the real position of Pyramid Rock and the true size of the indentation. We stayed very close in to the shore all the way along Tom's Beach, a long shingle shore to East Point, and then shot a spare line of traps for *Hilary* to pick up the following day off the anchorage. Then we set course for Tristan; Inaccessible disappeared into the clouds and mist at about a quarter to midday. We had hoped to drop off some spare bait on Tristan but our midday 'sched' told us the harbour was impracticable so Peter decided to pass round the eastern side: Tristan in its turn disappeared from view at about quarter to three. The ship was on the automatic pilot at nine and a half knots with fifteen hundred miles to go.

Peter Walker came on 'sched' to tell us that it had been snowing in North Yorkshire that morning, a new which failed to impress us very much as that was the evening when we saw the Grey-headed Albatross.

Round about midnight we passed a ship, a South American 'container' going from Hong Kong to South America. I couldn't sleep at all and joined Peter on the bridge very early on the morning of the 10th, my own Peter's birthday. (The Tristan PO, no doubt nagged by Marie-José, had faithfully done their stuff, as I later discovered.) All my personal worries were gradually disappearing, backed up as I was by Peter Warren's knowledge of the South Atlantic and the ham operating skills of both Peters, not to speak of the solid support of Bernard Hill, who was clearly playing a blinder in Cape Town. I was still desperately worried about the predicament of the remaining seven on Inaccessible because I knew that apart from the supply situation, which was due to get critical by the end of December, it would be a great psychological blow if they were not taken off for a Christmas break. I think it was that morning that I suggested to Peter that we might offer £5 per crew member involved in bringing the Expedition back, but he rightly observed that there was no way that this could be done tactfully since the Islanders had already promised to go on the first suitable day. His wisdom on that score did nothing to quieten my worries, which were aggravated when I heard on the radio that it was yet another non-fishing day on Tristan.

With us it was hazy for most of the morning but we forged along at just over nine knots and Peter opined that she should easily make Cape Town for the 16th, if not the 15th. I did some more paperwork in the Captain's cabin, having failed to persuade Richard that a change of scenery on the bridge might be good for him: I have suffered from seasickness several times in the North Sea and know that there is nothing more miserable, so I hope he didn't think I was unsympathetic. Then I went back to watch a mysterious brown petrel/shearwater which baffled me completely, though I have since realised that it must have been a White-chinned Petrel and that I hadn't noticed the white chin. (For obvious reasons we left all the ornithological books with Mike.)

I was joined on the bridge by Brian and Heather Kyles and their small boy, Gavin, the other expatriate family going home. I heard more tales of experiences on Tristan and one in particular which explained why Captain Leith had been in such a tearing hurry to get away in early November and why we never got our extra supplies via *Agulhas*. At tea-time we had a beer and I had a sudden vision of what Captain Leith might have said and done if he had found three passengers supping beer from cans on the bridge of the *Agulhas* at 4.30 pm. The possibilities seemed so horrific that I felt constrained to offer a second round from my dwindling supply, particularly as by that time it was very hot.

It continued hot all evening and all night: Richard and I opened cans of beer at midnight because it was impossible to sleep and by 4 am I was back on the bridge with Peter. Dawn came at about 4.30 and at 6 I saw an immature Wanderer, a sighting which Peter confirmed about a second later. At the 8 am 'sched' with Tristan the sun was glorious, by which time we were about 380 miles from them, but by 9 it had clouded over again: we learnt during the transmission that they had thirty knot winds gusting outside the harbour and that it was another non-fishing day.

What became evident during the course of the 11th, as I was shifting from bridge to deck, from deck to galley and from galley back to cabin (because there wasn't very much going on and the men were busy painting ironwork, which made bird-watching from the stern impossible) was that, as on the 'Agulhas,' the passengers and crew continued to regard Richard and me as 'the crazy ones.' The only difference was that on the *Agulhas*, everybody had become convinced that we were endeavouring to accomplish the impossible, whereas now, on *Tristania II*, everybody's attitude was tinged with admiration because of what the Expedition had already done. They still thought we were mad. The first mate, Redvers, had made his opinion quite clear on that first afternoon as we left Tristan - "You're those fucking crazy bastards who took schoolboys to Inaccessible!" he had said, and though we had had reservations about at least two-thirds of his terminology, we had pacifically agreed with the basic definition and had got on very well with him from then on.

Bird-watching from the bridge in the afternoon was par for the course and would probably have driven any 'birder' from the northern hemisphere mad with envy but after an hour I decided to watch a video film in the galley. It was called *Straw Dogs* and I still feel pangs of shame that I should have endured it rather than have remained on the bridge... However I got back there by half-past four and later listened in to many of Peter's ham friends transmitting: we did not intervene because whenever Peter started to transmit, the automatic pilot clicked like a Yellow-nosed Albatross simultaneously hatching an egg and resisting intruders.

I went to bed early and we left the door ajar, which made things a lot cooler so I slept for at least six hours consecutively, a rare event since 16 September.

On Sunday the 12th, I adopted my 'early shower' strategy and didn't arrive on the bridge until just after 6 am.

"Hello, John," said the Captain. "How's Rigor Mortis this morning?"

A little belatedly I realised that he was referring to my unfortunate companion and not to myself. I made noises on Richard's behalf but got a rather frosty stare when I asked the gallant Captain how many times HE had suffered from mal de mer.

As responsibility fell from my shoulders I was learning to take advantage of my unique opportunities. For hours each day and night I would stand on the bridge, surveying everything in front and keeping a wary eye behind. I was longing to spot a Taiwanese or Japanese 'long-liner,' a boat which lies very low in the water and whose fishing-lines could extend over thirty miles, according to Peter Warren. In the rear, I was on the look-out for a giant tanker or container-ship which could come up very fast behind and, as they too were on the automatic pilot, could give a little ship like the *Tristania II* a very nasty shock if not noticed well in advance. In neither direction were my efforts rewarded: the only time I saw 'long-liners' (which fished for tuna and shark) was in Cape Town harbour, and the only time I saw a big tanker was on the day we reached Cape Town, as it proceeded safely in a contrary direction, a mile away on our starboard bow.

My rewards in observations, zoological ones, were nevertheless enormous, as was my harvest of pieces of information from members of the crew and expatriates. It exalted my ego to learn that Stiubhard <u>still</u> could not understand how we had had the courage to land on Inaccessible when we didn't know how we were coming off and when I told him that the answer was pure ignorance he gave me an incomprehending look. Then I told him about the Abbé Siéyés who, when asked what he had done during the French Revolution replied, "J'ai survecu." I think he began to understand (Stiubhard, not the Abbé).

It was so pleasant to be welcomed at any hour of the day or night, usually with an enquiry as to whether one would like tea or coffee, even though the stewards learnt within twenty-four hours that I shared the Captain's (and James Bond's) anathema for tea. The same grey wastes of ocean extended before me but somehow they seemed bluer, the *Tristania II* was lower to the sea, the season was infinitely more mellifluous than October even though Rigor Mortis was still suffering; the menu was so incredible that the official Log on that day started as follows:

'Every time Richard and I sit down to one of *Tristania II*'s vast meals, we have a moment's pause while we think about the seven on Inaccessible - I spent most of the morning working out a food list for MKS to bring out from Cape Town, so I hope that by the time they come to read this, today's menus, pasted into the following pages, will not cause them any agonies ...'

My zoological observations continued that day when, having made 600 nautical miles by the log streaming from the stern by 8 am, I found that we had been joined a new passenger, an immature Antarctic Tern, looking very tired. So was I, but so must have been Libby, the devoted mother of three small children who were running about on the ship's decks for most of the daylight hours, so that was the afternoon when I volunteered to read to the two older ones while the little one was asleep. I don't know if they enjoyed four chapters of *Coot Club* as much as I did but it gave Libby a rest, even if she had to endure a video nasty in the galley.

Returning to the bridge at about 4 pm, I saw what looked like a prion just off the starboard bow: it seemed to have transparent wings and disappeared smartly into an advancing wave, a strange thing for a prion to do. I realised it was a flying-fish and twenty minutes later saw another, this time on the port side.

By this time, my diary says, the ship was rolling a good deal, though there was no rain ... She continued to roll throughout the night and I got up at 4 am to find that dawn had already broken. After an hour on the bridge, Peter muttered something and disappeared down the staircase. I glanced to my right, then to my left.

I was alone with six hundred and fifty tons of expensive equipment together with about forty human beings beneath my feet, forging remorselessly along at a steady nine and a half knots. What was interesting was that I felt exhilarated instead of apprehensive and I was quite happy when Peter reappeared about half an hour later.

"What was I supposed to do if anything went wrong?" I asked him.

His answer was the same as Andrew and Nelson's when I asked how I would find them in the tussock of the shearwater colony.

"Holler," he said.

The hour went forward because we had moved into another

time-zone and breakfast was early. It was a lovely sunny morning but Peter was concerned that the wind seemed to be shifting round to the south-east, even though there were 801 miles on the log at 6 am. There was still a lot of swell but Redvers put out deck-chairs on the fo'c'sle because there was fresh green paint everywhere else. Birdwatching was difficult because of the swell but I recorded the usual Stormies, Mollys and Wanderers, quite apart from a Sooty Shearwater, a Sooty Albatross and some more flying fish.

At about 6 pm, Peter decided that we ought to put out a call for Peter Walker because another 'ham' had reported that *Triple Hotel* had been trying to contact us. This meant switching off the automatic pilot and passing control to first mate Redvers.

"Keep her going on east-north-east," said Peter. "We'll only be away about half an hour."

"Got it," said Redvers. "East-south-east."

Without any change of inflexion, Peter said:

"No, east-north-east."

"Got it," said Redvers. "East-north-east."

It turned out that all *Triple H* wanted was a progress report. For once I went to bed early and Richard stayed up chatting with Stiubhard; the only time when we seemed to be in the cabin together was between midnight and 4 am!

Next day Rigor was definitely Mortis when I made my way up to the bridge at 5 am, even though the sea was flat calm and we were 'a painted ship, upon a painted ocean.' We moved on to Cape Town time, another hour forward at 8 am, at which moment we had just over three hundred miles to go. Good news, which I brought to RP who rolled over in his bunk, muttering "only three hours till lunchtime." I spent hours on the bridge and the stern but there were very few birds to observe apart from a Little Shearwater and a Great Shearwater, the latter obviously the Greta Garbo of the species, though it was heading west-south-west as if it wanted to make up for lost time.

I finished a long progress report for all DEI sponsors but had time to read a couple of paperbacks which caused Peter some alarm as I don't think he believed anybody could read a novel in two hours. On the bridge after dinner I was astonished to see a cloud of about two hundred miniature flying-fish jump out of the water about fifty yards away; Peter identified them as something he called 'Needle Fish.' I sat up late again with Stiubhard and Libby: in a funny way I think we were willing the voyage to go on longer because we knew the next day had to be the last.

I was up early on watch on Wednesday, the 15th, but there was nothing much to see. I stood on the bridge knowing that this had to be the end of the voyage and wondering why there was so little to observe.

Whatever happens, I thought, I will remember that once I saw albatrosses aloft, above the cliffs of Inaccessible at sunset, while twenty thousand shearwaters wheeled over the sea, and I was content.

It was 10.45 before half a dozen Great Black-backed Gulls swept across our wake but after that the bird-spotting was fast and furious. I quote from the official Log, which must be right ('Let history speak for itself' - pause - 'particularly as I' - pause - 'propose to write it!' W Churchill):

10.55, gannets. 11.00, Skua. 11.10, Antarctic Tern, two Wanderers, Yellow-nosed. 11.15, Sooty Shearwater, Great-winged Petrel. 11.35, White-chinned Petrel. 11.46, Giant Petrel. After lunch' (one has to have some sense of proportion)'Pintado, and from then on many gannets flying in perfect formation and huge flocks of cormorants. Land came into sight about 14.15 - at about 15.00 Peter spotted a (green) giant turtle solemnly swimming past the ship. Later we saw seals.'

As we came into Table Bay it was a source of some aggravation to our Captain that after a voyage of over three months he was obliged to give way to what he called "a bunch of fairies in yachts' who were racing in the bay. We were cheered by the sight of 'Agulhas' - a totally unexpected sight but there she was, setting forth to the Antarctic at that precise moment and having some difficulty in getting her helicopters on board. Despite his difficulties, Captain Leith found time to come through on the radio and enquire about the fortunes of the DEI. It gave me great pleasure to wish him 'Godspeed' as I watched his ship edging out to sea. We dropped anchor at 17.10 having made the voyage in the fast time of six days, one and a half hours. I talked to Peter Walker who congratulated me on my modulation and Peter Warren commented that the whole affair was "Naughty, naughty, naughty," but at least it brought people up to date with our movements.

We were not going to move into the dock that evening because Peter knew that if we did, his entire crew would disappear, get sozzled, and be totally useless for unloading next day.

The man arrived at 5 am, to say "Get up." I was, because I was anxious to get on the bridge whereas RP moved intelligently down to the galley and got himself a good breakfast while I was watching *Tristania II* come alongside with such precision that eggshells would not have cracked if they had replaced the fenders on the quay. It meant I missed breakfast. We started saying goodbye to different members of the crew and encountered apartheid when Redvers, shaking our hands, said
"I would like to invite you to my home while you are in Cape Town but the regulations don't allow me to ..."

The passport and customs officials checked us on the boat and Bernard Hill arrived to collect us. We said goodbye to Peter Warren whose cabin was full of his family and Bernard drove us to his home in Rondebosch where Brenda made us welcome and invited us to luxuriate in the bathroom, which we both did. For the next thirty-six hours the Hills surrounded us with kindness and attention: Bernard drove us along the coast of the Twelve Apostles to Lion's Head, the coast which we had been observing through the glasses as we moved in to Table Bay the previous afternoon. After a late lunch we then visited the beautiful old Cape Dutch town of Stellenbosch. At dinner that night we were encouraged to talk about our experiences and found we had an interested audience. Before we went to bed, I talked to Mike Swales in England and 'when I got to bed, it was far too comfortable after that damned bunk on *Tristania II* and I read a book about South Africa till 2 am.' (I quote my diary.)

We were driven into Cape Town the following morning, which we spent shopping, sight-seeing and cautiously deciding whether the pub where we wanted a beer was prepared to serve us. We were picked up by our old friend, Don McClachlan at the BP building and he took us to the Helmsley Hotel for a farewell drink with our expatriate 'compagnons de voyage,' before returning to Rondebosch with Bernard for a very late lunch served by the ever-tolerant Brenda. She then took us to buy presents in Claremont and showed us the Rhodes memorial.

We flew home that evening in a through flight to Heathrow with only a refuelling stop at Las Palmas with the usual courtesy and comfort of South African Airways. Bernard had exercised some kind of wizardry which put both of us on the same flight, even though our departure date had been put forward by one day. The story of our lives had become episodic: we did this, we did that, we went there, we went here, but we had some time to reflect about our experiences during that flight. When we finally got through baggage clearance at Heathrow next morning after the ritual hour and a half of standing about, we were met by Mike, Alison and Peter Pine-Coffin. I talked to Mike for thirteen hours and the next day he drove me home with my daughter, who had just stopped giggling every time she looked at my beard.

I see no need to write about the joys of either of those returns, even if I could, but I suppose I ought to try and answer the question which so many people have put to me as to why I went.

When I had said goodbye to the school on 29 September, I had quoted a line from Arthur Ransome's *We didn't mean to go to sea*:

"Grab a chance and you won't be sorry for a might-have-been."

My 'grab' had been made advisedly because I knew I needed a change but whether I had considered fully the responsibilities I was incurring is much more debatable. Somewhere in André Gide's *Si le grain ne meurt* he confesses the key phrase which

sums up his attitude to his life and work:
>'Nous devons tous représenter.'
>I hope I did.

Thursday, 13 January, 1983. Fyling Hall School. 1530 hours.
>Little boarders returning for new term.
Enter Raymond, meeting headmaster. "Hello, Grandad," he said.
>"Now listen," I started ...